McElroy hunts AFRICA

To John Ostrowski —
A very good friend &
a great guy.
All the best to you &
Barb. —

Sincerely Mac

Tucson AZ — Feb 15 1995

McElroy hunts AFRICA

by C. J. McElroy

A Sincere Press Publication published by
Sincere Press, Inc., Tucson, Arizona

Printed in the United States of America.
All rights reserved. No portion of this book may be reproduced in any form,
Mechanical or otherwise, without written consent.
© Copyright 1976, C.J. McElroy
Library of Congress Cataloging in Publication Data
McElroy, C.J.
  McElroy hunts Africa.
  1. Big game hunting--Africa. I. Title.
SK251.M153   799.2'6'096   76-17873
ISBN 0-912534-25-7
Designer: David L. Gurzenski
Printer: Automated Printing and Mailing, Inc., Tucson, Arizona

This book is dedicated to my wife, Alvie, without whose unselfishness and consideration, it could not have been written. Also, to those many men who I have met while hunting, who have helped me in many ways in acquiring my great collection of trophies.

Contents

Introduction	9
Foreword	11
A good beginning in Kenya	14
Taking tusks in Tanganyika	30
A return visit to Kenya	46
The elusive bongo of Kenya	66
Back in Kenya for bongo	90
The unspoiled land of the chad	100
Learning from mistakes in Mozambique	120
The ibex of Sudan	134
Ethiopia and its exotic animals	148
Tall tales in Angola	166
Breaking records in Southwest Africa	194
Zaire—different name, same game	208
Too late for trophies in Zambia	224
Air safari in Ethiopia	248
Success at a high price in Somali	266
Epilogue	272

Introduction

This book is dedicated to many people — to my wife, Alvie, without whose unselfishness and understanding, it never could have been written, and to all the top guides and outfitters in Africa with whom I have shared a hunt and campfire.

I was probably one of the last people born in a log house in the state of Texas. Great progress has been made since 1913 and the log houses went the way of the Dodo bird shortly after the turn of the century.

A boy born on a farm worked for his keep, and fifty years ago he probably worked more than he should have in the corn and cotton fields and cutting wood for the family. Yet with all the hardships of farm life, there were dividends that were dear to my heart. The opportunity to get into the forest with my dog to hunt was one of them.

The saddest years of my life were the few spent in the concrete jungles of a city. I feel very sorry for the man who has spent his childhood in a city never knowing the joy of hunting in the forest with his dog, or who has not spent hours just observing the wildlife without a thought of harming them.

Although I was born on a farm and familiar with the woods and wildlife almost from birth, my hunting career actually began one winter when I was nine years old. A "n'er-do-well" or somewhat shiftless man by the name of

Walter Prather invited me to accompany him as he ran his trap lines along the fork of the Denton and Elm Rivers in the County of Dallas.

To a nine-year-old boy who loved the woods this offer was very close to being asked to ascend straight to Heaven, and I am not sure what my choice would have been if given the alternative.

During that entire winter I trudged along behind Walter, helping him with the string of some one hundred traps, and skinning the animals after we had run the trap line. This experience of skinning was invaluable. In later years, I found that most of the time I could cape out and prepare the skin from an animal as well as the skinner on a safari and sometimes much better.

The next year, at the age of ten, I got my first gun — a 22 single shot Hamilton Rifle. That was the day I became a full-fledged hunter.

During the next thirty-five years, except for the war years, I never missed a season. I hunted everything from cottontail rabbit — our smallest game animals to moose — our largest. I hunted eighteen states including Alaska as well as Mexico, and five provinces of Canada. In those days I hunted for the sheer joy of the chase and of being in the forest and mountains. I was not interested in trophies and did not keep a single set of horns and antlers.

The start of my trophy hunts began in January of 1960 with my first trip to Africa. It was my initial hunting trip outside of North America, and the first of twenty-six separate African safaris in twenty-five different countries. Many unusual and interesting things happened on those shikars and safaris. This book is about those incidents.

Most sincerely,

C.J. McElroy

Foreword

I like to believe that I, as an outdoor writer, inspired C.J. "Mac" McElroy to publish accounts of his many African safaris as an informal educational text, just as he has inspired me and many other outdoorsmen to become true hunters, instead of just shooters.

But he has, and the result of my suggestions a decade ago is this book, "McElroy hunts Africa," which I, as a hunter, interpret as a how-to-do-it book, although to some readers who live the out-of-doors vicariously it may be an interesting, entertaining, exciting and well-illustrated volume. It is indeed both.

In this long-needed publication, McElroy, who has been acclaimed as the most experienced and authoritative contemporary big-game hunter in the world, gives us the inside on hunting in twenty-five of the most prominent and interesting countries of Africa. He has been there on twenty-six safaris and the fifteen chapters of his first book relate actual personal happenings within the Dark Continent which Mac has certainly helped to illuminate.

Some of the chapters were originally intended to be magazine articles, such as "Big Thicket Elephant" in which the author points out the importance of knowing where to place the bullet when confronted by a bull in heavy cover and when you are faced with the possibility of being crushed in the thicket by a charging pachyderm.

In other chapters this intrepid hunter tells of the habits and habitat of other dangerous big game such as the lion, rhino, buffalo, leopard and others; how to make an approach, to stalk and to move in on game, pitfalls to avoid, lessons learned, what rifles to use on various game and more—if you are to return alive and hunt another day.

In following "McElroy hunts Africa" it is evident that the author is a writer-hunter with guts, a keen observer and a naturalist as well.

An ever curious person, McElroy has sought game at elevations from sea level swamps to tops of 18,000-foot peaks. His motive was to learn intimately about the many strange species of animals which have fascinated him since boyhood.

McElroy, undeterred by obstacles, has often risked his life by pitting himself against nature's harshest elements and treacherous denizens of forbidden areas in order to collect 126 species. At all times he promotes the conservation of wildlife through selective trophy hunting of aged and infirm animals.

In presenting his findings in story form, McElroy appears to be different from other top hunters I have known. They, of course, know how to outwit game and to bag it intelligently but not all are as generous as Mac, who is willing to share the gained knowledge. Because of failure to communicate, their accomplishments and outdoor deeds often die with them, yet beginning sportsmen and newcomers to Africa might have benefitted from the costly discoveries.

Mac, on the other hand, passes on his African experiences as a heritage to the hunters of tomorrow. You will find the legacy in the next 272 pages.

Jim Brezina
Outdoor Editor
Los Angeles Herald-Examiner
Los Angeles, California

McElroy hunts AFRICA

A good beginning in Kenya

On my first safari in Africa I hunted with Glen Cottar, at that time a clean-shaven young man of 26. He is the son and grandson of professional white hunters in Kenya. In fact, I believe he is the only third generation white hunter in all of Africa.

We started the hunt in the Kiajiado area about 100 miles southwest of Nairobi. Two years later this land was made into a game reserve and closed to hunting.

It was a beautiful area, quite open, with plenty of grass and bush. The open area was dotted with big flat-topped Acacia trees that made ideal camping sites. There was plenty of game. Herds of Impala, Wildebeest, Grant and Tommy Gazelle, Zebra, a few Eland and some Oryx. The big five were well represented as well. We heard lions roaring every night. We saw elephants several times and a few buffalo. My hunting companion, Lee Williams, took a rhino in this area and it was here I shot my first leopard and lion.

A man's first leopard is always exciting even when nothing unusual happens, because this cat is not only the most beautiful of them all, but the most unpredictable and savage when aroused.

Preceding pages: Kenya proves to be the country to find the beautiful spotted leopard. Opposite: the full moon rises over the Kenyan plain and the lion comes out of hiding to hunt for food.

We put out 10 baits in the first three days of hunting, using Impala, Grant Gazelle and Warthog. Each morning we made the rounds and checked the bait. On the fifth day a leopard hit a bait.

A small blind was built of cut limbs and bushes about 40 yards from the tree where the partially eaten Impala hung. That evening, about an hour before sunset, Glen and I slipped quietly into the blind after walking about half a mile from where we had left the Land Rover.

This was my first night in a Leopard blind. No one who has not sat in a blind can really appreciate the feeling of tense excitement that is generated as you stare out through the small hole in the leaves and brush, straining your eyes for the first glimpse of the fierce spotted cat.

I would like to say the leopard came and I shot him from the tree — but he didn't come and my first try at a leopard failed. However, something interesting happened that I have not seen or heard of since that night.

The limb of the tree the bait was hanging from was silhouetted against the sky, but down below the shadows gathered quickly as the sun set until it was quite dark. We sat in complete silence, not moving a muscle. Only the chirps of the birds broke the stillness. Suddenly there was a rustle of leaves and a snap like the closing of a steel trap.

I looked at Glen; he was smiling to himself. Again the rustle and the snap! Glen leaned over and whispered in my ear: "It's a hyena jumping up, trying to get the meat."

The hyena jumped a few more times, then gave up and stillness descended once again, unbroken except for the twittering of birds as they moved to their resting places in the thicker bushes.

After complete darkness came we quietly left the blind and walked back to the Land Rover. The drive back to camp was made in silence; no one is happy when the leopard does not appear.

Two days later a leopard did come to the bait during a rainy afternoon when Glen and I were as wet as two drowned rats from a sudden downpour. I shot him through the neck as he lay in the fork of a tree with only a small portion of his upper chest and head exposed. He was a beautiful big tom with very small rosettes and ears that had been slit several times by other big cats in fierce battles.

I took one other of the "Big Five" in the Kiajiado camp: a lion, large in body but with a poor mane. This is often the case in Africa. The percentage of heavy maned lions is very small, perhaps one in a hundred. We had hung a wildebeest up for bait where another client of Glen's had killed a leopard a year earlier. The limb was not high off the ground and the tree grew on the edge of a shallow ditch or "Nulla" as it is called in Africa.

This bait was located close to camp and we checked it both morning and evening if we came back to camp before sundown.

One day we passed the bait about an hour before sundown. After stopping about a half mile from the tree, Glen, Lee and I approached the bait from the thick bushy side where the old blind had been built for the other client. Glen and I went into the blind while Lee waited outside.

I walked, stooped over to the front of the blind, and peeked out through the small hole that had been made to shoot through. I was somewhat startled to see a lion sitting on the edge of the Nulla facing me and staring at the blind. From the 30 yards that separated us I could see quite clearly the huge yellow eyes in the broad face.

There is something hypnotic about the eyes of any big cat. A lion's eyes are yellow or gold, quite different from the other big cats whose eyes range from a pale blue of the American Cougar to the dark green eyes of the leopard. If the soul of a man is reflected in his eyes, as it is often said, then the same can be said of the cats. I have never been able to look directly into the eyes of a big cat without feeling a cold chill pass through my body.

Even when a lion is lying under the shade of a tree with his belly full and content with the world, there is no friendliness in his eyes. He will stare at you with a bold defiant look until you approach too closely. Then the lips will form into a snarl around the big mouth and the eyes will change into golden pools of hate. I have never seen the eyes of a big cat reflect fear or terror as other animals do when cornered or frightened.

Glen nudged me. "Shoot him," he whispered. I put the cross hairs on his broad chest and squeezed the trigger.

The report of the 30-06 blended with the roar of the lion as he reared up and fell backward into the thick brush. Glen and I ran back through the blind to the entrance; he turned right and I turned to the left. I ran a few steps to the edge of the Nulla and looked down. There, standing broadside and looking at me, was a lion.

Without hesitation I raised my gun and shot him, hitting him in the back. He roared, turned toward me and I shot him in the head.

Over on the other side of the blind there was quite an uproar, with growls from another lion and several shots.

After making sure my lion was dead, I went around the blind where Glen and Lee were. There was no lion in sight. "He went into the bush there," Glen said. "Let's go get him."

If there is anything good about a wounded lion, it is the fact that he will let you know where he is at all times when you start into the bush after him. He will growl each time he hears movement. If you make him angry by throwing sticks or rocks into the bush, quite often he will charge out after you.

This is not true of the leopard, who will lie motionless behind a small clump of grass and brush until you are within a few feet of him. In one leap he will be tearing you to bits.

The three of us advanced in a line on the thick bush along the Nulla and the lion came out growling hoarsely. He was wounded very badly and could not move very fast but with the courage of his kind, he came to meet us to do battle. Two loads of buckshot from Glen's shotgun and a slug from Lee's 375 put him down to stay. I didn't fire; it was Lee's lion and I never interfere with another man's game unless I am asked or if the situation gets bad.

Shortly after the lion kill we packed up and left the Kiajiado area, trading the lovely flat-top Acacia trees and scattered bush for the thick tangled

The typical tent safari would never be featured in Better Homes and Gardens, but at the end of a long day's hunt, it was a comfortable place to rest.

jungle of vines, ferns and bamboo found on the slopes of Mount Kenya.

This was a two-day trek for us even though we covered less than 300 miles. There were very few paved roads in Kenya in those days and the road up the side of Mount Kenya was narrow and so steep in some places that we used the Land Rover to help get the big lorry through the bad spots.

The air grew colder as we moved up the mountain in late afternoon. At about 9000 feet we made camp just off the side of the dusty road. Giant trees towered above us; the moss hanging from the limbs and Colibus monkeys sitting in the branches with their long black and white tails hanging down behind them. They are the handsomest of all monkeys, with their black and white faces and the apron of long white hair hanging down over the back of their hips.

This was the jungle that one reads about. Big trees cutting out the sun, large vines and creepers, thick stands of bamboo impossible to walk through, and alive with animals.

There were elephant, rhino, buffalo and leopard, to name four of the big five on this mountain, not to mention exotic game like the bongo bushbuck and yellow back duiker. The rare giant forest hog and bush pig could also be found. We set up camp and built a big campfire. The night was cold, and through the foliage of the overhanging trees, millions of stars twinkled in the clear sky.

We hunted for eight days on Mount Kenya and each day was an adventure in itself. Not a day passed that we were not scared by a rhino or elephant. Many times it was not the fault of the animal but the condition under which the meeting between man and animal took place.

The problem was the dwarf bamboo that grew on the side of the mountain. This bamboo grew to a height of 10 to 20 feet and was so thick that only the large animals such as the giant forest hog, rhino and buffalo could penetrate it. They had made tunnels through this bamboo which looked exactly like a mine tunneled through a mountainside. If you wanted to hunt this area it was impossible to do so without going into these tunnels, because the bamboo sometimes covered two or three acres of ground.

Before entering a tunnel, we always listened carefully at the entrance for the sound of an animal occupying that patch of bamboo. However, sometimes the rhino, buffalo or elephant were lying down resting and we couldn't hear them. Many times we ran back the way we had come when the animals started snorting and crashing through the bamboo.

Most of the time we just froze in the tunnel with guns ready, and waited until all was quiet or the animal roared past us in another tunnel nearby. It was very dangerous hunting, not because the animals wanted to hurt us, but because in the thick brush they could not see us until too late. In the case of rhino coming down the same tunnel there would be no place for us to go. At the age of 26 years, Glen Cottar had a lot of nerve. I am quite sure an older man would have hesitated before taking two greenhorns into those bamboo patches.

I shot a good rhino on Mount Kenya with a horn length of 22 inches front and 17 inches rear. Lee Williams took a good buffalo. Then we came down and headed for what many professional hunters think is the best elephant country in all of Africa — along the Tana River in the northern frontier country.

The road to Garrisa, on the Tana River, is a long thin ribbon that snakes its way across the red sandy desert, from the green hills and cultivated land around Nanyuki to the harsh, sunbaked desert land of the Somalis.

This is a hard country and water is scarce during the dry season. In the wet season, April-May and October-November, this land becomes waterlogged and traffic ceases between the two towns. In fact, the elephant herds find it hard to move in the heavy mud, sometimes sinking over two feet at each step.

Like most deserts there is quite a lot of wildlife. Tremendous flocks of vulterine guinea fowl stand in the skimpy shade of the scrub trees along the road. Small antelope called Dik-Dik flash across the road or stand watching you curiously as you pass. There are beautiful Lesser Kudu with spiral horns and ivory tips. Hunters Hartebeest and herds of Oryx are to be found in this dry, arid land.

Just before we really got started into the desert country, we passed through the small town of Isiola. Here we were stopped by the villagers and asked to go and kill an elephant that had killed a local man. Lee and I were all for it but Glen explained that we would have to have permission from the Game Department before we could act.

We reluctantly moved on and a short time later saw four bull elephants some distance from the road. We discussed the possibility that one of them was the killer elephant.

We camped that night on the desert and the next day we reached Garrisa. We passed several bands of Somali in the desert. The tall, arrogant men dressed in bright robes and sandals, while their women wore plain black robes and kept the lower part of their faces covered. The Arabic influence is strong in this area. The people have Arabic features, i.e., thin lips and a high bridged nose. They are extremely warlike. A few years after I hunted here, the entire area, from Isiola to the border of Somali, was closed.

There is no place in all Africa where one can see more elephants than along the Tana River. This wide muddy river starts in the highlands around Mount Kenya, drops down across the desert and empties into the Indian Ocean. It is the only river of any magnitude for several hundred miles through the desert country and the elephants depend on it for water. For centuries they have lived along its banks, drinking its muddy water and feeding on the bushy plants that sprinkle the land. They graze away from the river for a day or two, then graze back to the river to drink.

The best way to hunt elephants in this country is to drive along the bank of the river and look at the tracks, or spoor, as the professionals call them. When you find one 22 inches or better across, this is an animal worth looking over.

Many times in the next eight days we followed big spoor only to find a big bull with one or two broken tusks. Sometimes the elephants were just not big enough and we were not interested.

Glen Cottar, my first professional hunter in Africa, became a good friend and frequent companion on other safaris to the Dark Continent.

Early one morning we followed five bulls out from the river. About 8 o'clock we were still going, but then we lost them in a large herd of cows, calves and other bulls.

We were pretty well bushed and disgusted, so we stopped to rest under one of the very few skinny trees in the area. We had just finished drinking from a canteen when three tall Somali warriors popped out of the bush. It was sheer magic; however, I have seen this happen many times since then. You can be out in the forest or desert, many miles from the nearest settlement or manyatta. You stop to either eat or drink. Suddenly they are there, coming silently out of the bush to stand and stare at you. It's my opinion that quite often these warriors follow hunting parties out of curiosity just as an animal will often do. If he wants to show himself, he will and if not, you never will see him.

Quite often this same thing happens when you kill a large animal. Suddenly the natives are there waiting to take the meat.

We were happy to see these fellows as they told us about seven bulls they had just seen. We gave them water (I knew they must have been 25 miles from the river) and they led us back through the bush toward the river, walking along with effortless five-foot strides.

We came upon the bulls in a few minutes. They were standing under a pair of skinny trees in two groups, five under one tree and two under the other. We stopped about 200 yards away to study the ivory.

Pissy, Glen's gun boy, methodically tapped a small bag of ashes every few minutes to check the wind while Glen and I discussed the elephants in whispers.

"There's only one that's worth taking," Glen said, "That big bull in the group of five, I think he will go about 85 pounds and he's very even."

That was all I needed and in the 120-degree heat we began to maneuver around so I could get a shot without wounding one of the others. We walked slowly toward the elephants with no cover at all. They cannot see you 50 yards away if you move slowly. Most of them stood absolutely still except for the gigantic ears that waved slowly back and forth. Two or three rocked gently on their huge, flat-bottomed feet. The only noise was an occasional gurgle from the bellies of the giant pachyderms.

Fortunately, the bull we wanted stood facing out from the group, his head and shoulders in the clear. He was about eleven feet high at the shoulder and the closer I came to him, the bigger he looked. At about 35 yards, Glen and I stopped and he whispered, "Now."

I settled the front bead of the .458 in the vee of the rear sight, lined it up on the shoulder and squeezed off.

The blast of the shot was followed with squeals of anger and fright from the elephants as the red dirt churned. The five broke for the bush but not until I had put another solid shot into the body of the elephant I had hit. He followed the herd about 100 yards and began to weave, then collapsed in a huge cloud of red dust.

He was still moving a bit when we walked up to him. I administered the coup de grace by shooting him in the back of the head into the brain. Thus ended my first elephant hunt — a thrilling experience.

The camp on the Tana River was one of the prettiest places in which I have ever camped. It was an old plantation that had been left unattended since the death of the man who had settled there at the turn of the century. He left his mark in the savage country by planting mango, banana and other fruit-bearing trees before departing.

No evidence of buildings were present. If there had ever been anything of a permanent nature, it had long since been destroyed by both time and the elements. The only building that can survive long in Africa is either stone or concrete and I am sure no concrete was available on that lonely stretch of muddy river, over a thousand miles from any town, some seventy years ago.

Glen said an Englishman had settled there alone and lived for many years. I couldn't help but think of this man as I lay on my cot in the shade of the big mango tree in the middle of the day. The heat was stifling and I reckoned it was over 120 degrees in the shade and much more in the sun.

What manner of man would settle on this river so many miles away from any of his kind? What was he seeking and did he find what he sought? I like to get away from people occasionally and have done so often in my lifetime, but to bury yourself as this man had done was inexplicable to me. Anyway, he had done so and created a lovely spot on the river bank and we were happy to take advantage of the fruits of his labor.

I also took a buffalo while staying in this camp but the horns were not impressive. I would never have taken him if he had not stood in the thick brush watching Glen and I as we walked along the trail. That was a mistake on his part. Glen saw him and we didn't know what his intentions were, so I shot him before he could make up his mind.

Yet we had come to the Tana River to hunt elephant and we had taken two tusks that were 7 feet 10 inches and 7 feet 11 inches long. Beautiful slender sticks of ivory are hard to come by in Africa today. So we folded our tents, loaded up the big lorry and left the lovely, green spot on the river to the ghost of the unknown settler.

We again crossed the desert, stopping briefly at Grissa to weigh the ivory and found them to be 89 and 90 pounds, not as heavy as I would have liked but long, lovely ivory nonetheless.

Our next and final camp on the safari was at a small stream called "The Garba Tula," located about 50 miles out of Isiola. It was just at the edge of the desert and many species of animals — both desert and bush — came to water at the large swamp where the stream ended, and went underground.

The country was quite open except for some "whistling" thorn trees and

My first elephant was taken in the northern frontier country in Kenya and had an impressive set of tusks.

some huge thickets of "wait-a-bit" thorn. The whistling thorn gets its name from the round seed pods that hang in the tree like black walnuts with thorns protruding from all sides. The huge black ants of Africa chew holes in the pods, eat the seeds and leave the empty shell. When the wind blows — and it does often in this area — the pod produces a shrill whistle, hence the name whistling thorn.

The wait-a-bit thorn bush got the name from having thorns like a cat's claws. Thousands of curved thorns cover every inch of the branches and leaves. When a person brushes against this bush and gets entangled, it's impossible to pull away without tearing both flesh and clothes, so wait-a-bit is a good name for it.

We set up camp on the little stream under some large trees and went out to look the area over. We saw many animals right away: Gerenuk, Grant

Gazelle, Impala, the most beautiful species of giraffe — the Reticulated Giraffe, and rarest of zebra — the Grevy.

It was also a good area for wild fowl. We saw hundreds of Franklin Grouse (common name — Yellowneck), many flocks of both common and Vulterine Guinea fowl, and we disturbed several pair of Sand Grouse squatting in the sand who took off with a blast of their pointed wings. Last and the least, small Button Quail about the size of a golf ball, fluttered up out of the grass, flew a few feet, then dropped back into the grass again. The place was alive with game.

We returned to camp just at sunset. Right after we arrived, a lone bull elephant with about 40 to 50 pounds of ivory walked almost into camp. Walking downwind, he didn't scent us until he was almost upon the camp. The boys had seen him come out of the bush and stopped talking to see how near he would come.

He grew uneasy about 100 yards from the camp — stopped, flopped his ears and raised his trunk. Someone slapped his hand against metal, the old boy wheeled and rolled away. All the boys laughed; it was a good joke on old Jumbo.

A very exciting incident happened in that camp. We needed a buffalo for myself and a leopard for Lee Williams. We spent the first day putting up baits for the cat, then went back to camp early, about 3 o'clock. When we arrived we saw that we had company — four Somali warriors.

Glen talked to them and after some discussion turned to me and said: "This chap says that he can show us some buffalo right now, very close by."

We didn't have much time left to hunt, but decided to give it a try. All four Somalis, our two gun boys, Kuttetette, Pissy, Glen and I climbed in the Land Rover and headed down toward the swamps.

Leaving the driver with the vehicle we stopped at the edge of the swamp, crossed over a small stream and started climbing a small hill dotted with big patches of "wait-a-bit" thorn.

We were walking alongside a large patch of this thorn bush, when suddenly we came upon a cow buffalo and a half-grown yearling grazing in an open space between the thorn bushes.

She turned to look at us, then without further movement, wheeled around and came straight for us in a charge. Both Glen and I shot her in the chest by the time she had covered half the 20 yards that separated us. This didn't stop her. She uttered a grunt and came on like a black runaway locomotive. Glen shot again, using the second barrel of his .500, causing the old cow to crumple in a sliding halt at our feet. The yearling veered off to the right when the cow fell.

I took three steps and my foot touched her nose. Small drops of blood trickled slowly from a hole almost exactly between her eyes. Glen's second shot, at very close range, had done the job and put a bullet into her brain. Had his bullet hit any other place, she would have been on us. There was no place to go as we were backed up against the "wait-a-bit" thorns.

Glen stepped over, patted her shoulder and said, "You silly old bitch, you wouldn't be dead if you hadn't charged us."

We examined the buffalo and found that one horn had been knocked loose and that there were worms down in her head. She must have been crazed with pain most of the time. This was the first and last time I ever saw a horn broken loose from the skull of a buffalo. It must have taken a terrific blow to knock it loose.

In the same area on the Garba Tula we took Grevy Zebra, Northern Grant Gazelle, Kirk's Dik-Dik, Gerenuk, Impala and Warthog. Lee also collected his leopard and I shot a good buffalo in the seven-foot reeds that grew along the edge of the swamp.

It was also an exciting kill as we had to trail the buffalo through the tall reeds without seeing him until we suddenly came on the animal.

I shot him once and he ran away through the tall reeds. We followed slowly and were fortunate to quickly find an anthill about three feet high. I climbed up on it and looked over the tops of the reeds. Fifty feet away, the old bull stood waiting for us with blood streaming down his shoulder. I shot again from the anthill and he dropped in about six inches of water. Thus ended my first safari in Africa.

2

Taking tusks in Tanganyika

One year later, I found myself back in Africa for another hunt with Glen Cottar. It was March, and Nairobi looked just the same; a sleepy, placid town. Much of its local color came from the native Africans and three other races: the Arabs that have been in Africa for hundreds of years, and the late arrivals, the English and the Indians. The combination created a hodge-podge of architecture styles. Most of the buildings were of early British design, while a sprinkling of structures showed a distinct Arabic and Indian influence. A beautiful mosque with a golden roof right in the center of the town was a perfect example.

The new Stanley Hotel was the jumping-off place for people on safari. One could always find some eager novice big game hunter sitting in the long bar, having a drink with his professional hunter or out in the open area near the front door called "The Thorn Tree" having coffee, or a bit of lunch while watching the many different types of people go by.

Upstairs in the dining room, black waiters in long white robes and red fezzes on their heads padded silently about, bearing large trays of wonderful food. This was Nairobi in the late fifties and early sixties.

Glen picked me up in a Land Rover in front of the hotel the next

Preceding pages: This grazing elephant carries about 60 pounds of ivory.
Opposite: Measuring the tusks is an exciting moment after taking a large elephant.

morning. Behind him was the huge lorry, loaded high with camping gear, supplies and 10 men perched on top like magpies. Going on safari was still a big thing in Nairobi and everyone enjoyed the excitement.

We drove about 200 miles that day and stopped early to set up camp for the night. We were going down into Tanganyika to hunt sable, kudu and anything else that looked good. We heard lions roaring during the night on this, the main road from Nairobi to Tanganyika.

We traveled another day and came into colorful Tabora, the former capitol of Tanganyika under the German rule. The town was almost 100 percent black. There were a few Indians, but the only white face seen during the time spent there was at the Game Department.

While we were getting our licenses and game permits, most of the boys disappeared. The next three hours were spent in rounding them up and getting them back on the lorry.

We traveled southwest out of Tabora. The ending dry season had left the land parched and in need of water. All the small streams and ponds had dried up. We came to the Kilulu River and found it empty. We drove along the bank for about 30 miles and found a muddy pool where the river had been the deepest. We made camp on the bank overlooking the brown water.

We were in the Miambo Forest. The trees were not very big but quite thick. Most were not more than eight inches at the base. The leaves on the bushes were burned crisp, and what grass there was was dry and yellow.

While the boys set up camp, we checked the slimy mud around the stagnant pool, looking at the tracks left by animals. There were many different sets of tracks: kudu, roan, impala, zebra and hartebeest. The big cats had also watered there. We saw both lion and leopard spoor.

It was dark before we sat down to eat but the heat still hung like a hot blanket around us. That night I slept with all sides of the tent rolled up in order to get a little air.

Next morning I was awakened by the sound of women's voices behind my tent. After slipping on my pants and my camp boots, I went out to see who they were. Five big native women, bare to the waist, were laughing and talking to Cottar's gun boy, Pissy. Each woman had a large clay pot on her head that had been filled from the pool. Their legs were covered with mud up to the bottom of their skirts and, no doubt, beyond their knees. They were a happy lot and I got the feeling by listening to the talk that Pissy was trying to date one of them. Their eyes twinkled as they talked and giggled with him.

I looked at the smelly pool where they had gotten the water and gave a silent thanks to the people who had invented the water filter that we were using. We were drinking the same water that the natives and animals were wading in.

We spent the next five days looking for sable and kudu. There were not many around. We saw quite a few other animals but nothing like the herds of game found in Kenya on my first trip.

I did take one sable with horns of 39 inches during that time; also some lesser game of oribi, hartebeest, impala, and roan. We had heard lion grunting and growling down at the pool one night and wanted to get a look at the pride. Both the sable and roan were hung up for lion bait.

The next morning we checked the roan with no success. Then we drove the five miles that separated the two baits and stopped about a half mile away from where the sable hung. Glen and I made the approach by coming up behind a giant ant hill. We looked over the top and saw five lions — four females and a big male.

There was very little left of the sable. The backbone hung from the hips like a huge string of beads. Both leg bones were attached to the backbone and a lioness was standing on her hind legs working the bones as they swayed from side to side.

The old male had a pretty fair mane, most of it black. He lay on his full belly with his eyes closed. I shot him in the shoulder and he just rolled over and twitched a few times before lying still.

"Shoot him again," Glen said. "Why?" I asked. "He's dead." "Shoot him again or I will," he said. So I shot the lion again.

He didn't move, but at the second shot two of the females growled and started walking around, switching their tails while the other two remained content under the shade of a tree.

"Put a shot just under that closest one facing us," said Glen. I carefully put a shot between her feet. The dirt flew up and she growled, jumped around and ran off toward the thick bush. The other three followed slowly.

Glen and I stood up and shouted at them. This sent them loping to the bush where they disappeared a moment later.

The lion was huge. Glen thought it was the biggest he had ever seen. He was so curious about the weight of the beast that he decided to try to weigh him.

The view from the new Stanley Hotel offers a glimpse of the bustling city of Nairobi in 1959.

The only scale we had in camp would weigh up to 100 pounds and necessitated cutting up the lion in sections. The task accomplished during the heat of the day was, without a doubt, the most miserable job we could have undertaken. The stench from the cat's intestines was terrible and caused the entire camp to smell.

The lion weighed 443 pounds. Because of the weight of the lost blood, we felt he would have weighed over 450 pounds intact. I sure wouldn't want to try weighing another one piece by piece. We were happy to have the boys take the animal into the bush downwind and leave it.

I took a very interesting specimen on this trip—a Monitor Lizard over six feet long. The lizard looked like a miniature prehistoric animal out of The Stone Age. It was a rare encounter and the only one I have ever seen on safari.

The drought brought other animals and reptiles down to the water hole. One morning I killed a nine-foot python that had come in search of water.

On the sixth day in the camp on the Kilulu, we returned for lunch and found we had royal visitors, Prince Wilhelm of Liechtenstein and his daughter, Margaret. They were sitting under the shade of the dining room tent, drinking squash in tall glasses filled with crushed ice.

Edgar de Bono, the professional white hunter of their safari, had hunted in the Kilulu River area before and, unaware of our party, had brought the Prince in search of game. Because our camp was located at the only water hole within the large region, they had come to request permission to share it with us.

Permission, of course, was granted and they set up camp on the other side of the river about half a mile away. The Prince proved to be a likeable, old gentleman in his late sixties with a keen love of hunting. His family has always been hunters. The Liechtenstein Hartebeest was named after his uncle. I showed him the trophies I had collected and he was very impressed with the Monitor Lizard. It was the first one he had seen. He mentioned that he would like to take one for the Liechtenstein Museum.

I offered him the one I had taken. He seemed quite pleased that a hunter would give up a valued trophy to someone he didn't know very well. He would accept it only if he did not take one himself. Two days later he shot a smaller lizard which made him very happy.

One night we were invited to have dinner with the Prince and Margaret. While eating we were discussing women going on safari. The Prince was very much opposed to the idea and I could tell he regretted having his daughter accompany him.

The food was excellent. We were on the main course when Countess Margaret gave a little scream and almost knocked the table over trying to get her feet up into her chair.

All four men rushed around to see what she was staring at on the floor. Crawling along past the legs of her chair was a big hairy tarantula about six inches wide. He was a sight to upset almost anyone if encountered unexpectedly.

The old Prince gave a grunt of disgust, jumped on the giant spider with both feet and squashed him flat. Then with a look of disdain directed at his daughter, he returned to the head of the table.

"That," he said, "is the reason I don't like women on safari. They get upset too easily." The dinner was finished in an embarrassed and strained atmosphere. I, for one, felt the old boy was a little rough on his daughter.

We hunted two more days on the Kilulu River, then loaded up, bid the Prince and Countess goodbye and left the area. We drove northeast toward dark storm clouds that were gathering on the horizon. We were expecting the short rains which come during late March and continue through the first part of May. The long dry season was coming to a close.

It was raining when we arrived in Tabora. We spent the night in the Tabora Hotel, a relic built during the colonial days when the Germans settled Tanganyika.

The next morning we left in bright sunshine and proceeded south toward Iringa, a small town near the center of Tanganyika.

On the way we passed huge sisal plantations that had been carved out of the wilderness by the German pioneers in the late 18th and early 19th centuries. Most of the plantations were deserted and the sisal was going to seed. Old dilapidated buildings were falling down from dry rot as the jungle was slowly but surely reclaiming the land.

We set up camp below Iringa, an all black village. Glen sent men into town in search of eggs and chickens. They returned with the supplies and two local hunters who would guide us while we were in the area.

The tsetse flies were bad and bothered us all day until nightfall. The bite is like jabbing a small hot pin into your flesh and will itch for a short time after you are bitten. Like most flies, they are especially active just before a rainstorm or shower. We suffered a bit from the fly.

We were hunting for a better kudu than I had killed earlier in the safari. We also hoped to find a large elephant. Some big ones have come out of Tanzania.

Two days later we were driving along a track when one of the boys called out that he could see elephant spoor. Checking the spoor we found that five bulls had just recently crossed the pathway. It was very hard to see the fine lines the huge flat feet had left on the hard ground. The largest print measured over 20 inches.

After a short discussion we decided to follow the herd to see what the ivory looked like. We started out on the trail, leaving Malaffo, the driver, and one boy to find a way to follow us in the Land Rover. We walked for about three hours, following a trail of broken limbs pulled from trees and small trees that the bulls had pushed over to reach the top green foliage.

We came to a peculiar grove of bushes, trees and vines that are native to some parts of Tanganyika. These groves are called "thickets" and well deserve the name. The only place I have seen such dense brush was on the slopes of Mount Kenya where bamboo thickets grew. Once the decision was made to go into a thicket you had to follow the trails made by elephants.

Glen asked me if I wanted to go after the elephant and I answered in the affirmative. Pissy took off his clothes and shoes and hung them on a bush. Then attired only in a pair of shorts, he led the way into the thicket following the fresh trail of the bulls.

The sun was immediately blotted out by the foliage overhead, but that did not matter. Clouds were beginning to roll in from the northeast as the rumble of thunder sounded like distant drums. There was not a breath of air stirring in the thicket; it was like going into an oven.

The four of us moved forward very slowly — Pissy, Glen, and I, followed by my gun boy, Kuttette. I wondered if Pissy would ever again see the shoes and clothes he had left behind.

In the distance the muffled crack of a limb being torn off a tree came to our ears. Glen raised his hand and we stopped to listen. The sound was not repeated and we moved forward again. We had gone about two hundred yards into the thicket when Pissy stopped dead still, put his finger to his lips and pointed forward.

I couldn't see anything. I don't believe Glen could either. He motioned Pissy forward and stepped aside to allow me to go in front of him. Slowly we eased forward again another 10 yards. Then the unmistakable burp and belly rumble of an elephant's stomach sounded to our right. All of us turned and there he was, screened by the bushes, standing half asleep not more than 20 feet away.

I looked at Glen for instructions. He brought his binoculars up quickly to his eyes, hoping to see better through the screen of leaves and brush. I waited as a few drops of rain started to fall. Glen carefully lowered his binoculars down on his chest, made a circle with his two hands to indicate the size of the ivory and nodded his head. "Shoot him," he said noiselessly.

I raised the .458 and shot the elephant in the head. It was not a good shot because I had to shoot through the screen of leaves. He paused a moment and I thought he would go down. Then he lurched forward and I shot him again, this time in the chest cavity.

At the sound of the second shot, the thicket exploded with elephants running in all directions. We quickly stepped into a small clearing a few feet wide and waited. A bull came crashing toward us. Pissy couldn't stand the pressure and tore off through the bush, dodging like a rabbit. The bull came to a stop about 20 feet from us with ears flared and trunk up. Glen and I waited with rifles raised. Kuttette stood directly behind me, steady as a rock. As the bull tested the air a flash of lightning lit up the thicket, thunder crashed and he bolted off in another direction.

We stood in the little clearing another 15 minutes while we heard elephants pass several times. There must have been more than five elephants in that thicket unwilling to go out into the open forest and face the storm. The wind had begun to swirl about the brush, causing the animals to be further disturbed by our scent.

We waited a short time after we heard the last elephant move, then went over to where I had shot the bull. There was no blood, but that didn't surprise us. Generally, a wounded elephant will not leave blood on the ground. Finally we found blood on the bark of a tree and on leaves of the bushes as we slowly took up his trail.

We had gone about 20 yards when we heard a whistle. Glen and Kuttette stopped and looked at each other. Kuttette grinned, showing where his two front teeth were missing, typical of the Wacumba tribe. When Glen nodded his head, Kuttette whistled a reply.

A few moments later Pissy came into view with his eyes averted and a downcast expression on his face. His body showed evidence of his flight through the thicket. Blood seeped from cuts and bruises on his chest and legs. A lump blossomed on his forehead where he had run into a limb. I felt sorry for the little fellow as Glen harangued him in Swahili. I, too, had felt like running but didn't know where to go.

We returned to tracking the bull and found him dead a short distance away. We cut off the tail and retraced our way to where we had entered the thicket. Continuing to backtrail, we met the Land Rover coming slowly along the trail. It had been a hard but exciting day.

The next morning Glen and I slept in, then had a late breakfast. This was ivory collecting day and we would not be hunting. After we finished breakfast, Glen called Pissy over, directing him to take four men and the driver to collect the ivory from the elephant I had shot. Pissy informed him that one of the men, Marteniz, could not go because he was sick. When asked what was wrong, Pissy replied: "Mango Flies."

"Are you sure?" asked Glen.

"I am sure," Pissy replied. "I just took the larva out of him."

I asked Glen what they were talking about and he explained that in this area there was a fly called a "Mango Fly" that would sting a man or beast and deposit an egg underneath the skin. Within a few days the egg would hatch into a larva which would feed on the person or animal until developing into an adult fly.

I reminded Glen I had complained of several itching spots on my back and shoulders. He had not bothered to check the places, saying I had scratched some tsetse fly bites.

"Pull your shirt off and let's look at your back," he said.

I pulled my undershirt over my head and turned my back to him.

"I'll be damned," he said. "They really got to you."

It was a painful experience having the larva taken out of my body. It was done by pressing both thumbs very hard against the swollen boil where the larva lay. The force of the pressure caused the larva to pop out the small opening in the skin through which the egg had been deposited. Some of the larvae were a half inch long. Under the reverse end of binoculars, the larva could be magnified many times. They resembled the larvae of a wasp except for the short black hair on the body and oversized pinchers in the head.

We reckoned Mango flies had bitten me during the heat of the day while I

A Somali woman fills her buckets with water from the Tana river behind a brush barrier.

lay on a cot under a shade tree attired only in shorts. I gave Glen a bad time about not looking after his client when I complained about the terrible itching and the insects eating me alive.

The rains came soon after I killed the elephant. Not the light rains we expected, but heavy rains that kept us in the tents for two days and nights. The dry hard earth turned to black mud that clung to everything. We went hunting and got stuck twice. Each night it would rain again until the land was soaked with water. We stuck it out another five days, then loaded up and started back for Tabora.

Two more days passed before we arrived in Tabora. The elephant tusks which we carried weighed 56 and 58 pounds, about average for Tanganyika. I lost track of the times we were bogged down. We had a winch on the front

of the Land Rover and the lorry that proved invaluable. Without them we would have had to give up. The small Land Rover was so light we could get enough manpower to lift in out of the bad spots.

At Tabora we abandoned the outfit and the two large vehicles. With the small Land Rover and three of the boys, we started for Mwanza, a good sized town with an airport located about 200 miles west on Lake Victoria.

We ran into floodwaters on the way but managed to reach a point within 25 miles of Mwanza. There we were stopped by a long line of waiting trucks and people where a wide stream of water was flowing across the road.

We maneuvered the small Land Rover up to the head of the line of trucks where Glen and I looked at the fast flowing stream of water. "What do you think?" he asked. "Looks rather swift," I said, "but not too deep. I

The heavy rains play havoc with the Land Rover and slow down travel through Tanganyika.

wouldn't drive across it, but if you want to try, I will walk ahead and check for washouts."

He agreed. While the people on both sides watched, I took off my shoes and pants, held hands with Malaffo, the driver, and started slowly into the water.

We had gone only about 10 yards when another Land Rover put out from the other side and started to cross. "What the Hell," Glen said. "If he is coming over, let's wait and see if he makes it."

The Land Rover moved further into the water with no one guiding it to check for holes. The front end bobbed as the tires dipped in washed-out places, then would level out and move forward. The driver was almost half way across when the right front wheel must have dropped into a deep hole. He tried to reverse but the weight of the vehicle and the force of the water sent him forward. The Land Rover started a slow, graceful roll away from the force of the water. A woman screamed as the Land Rover rolled over twice. Two Indian men popped out of the vehicle and pulled a woman out with them. The water was about four feet deep but they had to fight hard to make shore. The blacks were howling with laughter.

"Well, that does it," said Glen. "Maybe we can cross in the morning."

The next morning the water had receded to a small stream in the center. We hired enough men to physically carry the small vehicle across the bad spots in the road. An hour later we were in Mwanza.

We stayed the night in Mwanza, and in the morning flew back to Nairobi. I was expecting my wife, Alvina, to meet me there for a short 10-day safari in the Narok area of Kenya. She arrived a day later and it was a pleasure to show her the interesting sights of the town.

Glen borrowed safari equipment from his friend, Walter Jones, and again we set out on safari. It was still raining and flood waters were reported throughout East Africa. It was described as the heaviest rainfall in nearly 100 years. Bridges on main roads were swept away and safari outfitters were stranded in many locations.

We didn't travel far, only 80 miles from Nairobi to the Narok area where we set up camp and tried to ignore the rain.

We stayed eight days in this camp. Several leopard baits were put up and we shot some plains game; Grant and Tommy gazelle, topi, zebra and wildebeest. Alvina shot a record book warthog and kongoni which made her very proud, but she didn't have the heart for much killing.

She showed good spirit in spite of the bad weather and was interested in all that took place on the hunt. On the last day we had a leopard feeding, but had to cut the bait down and let him have it. We loaded up and headed for Nairobi, ending a 45 day safari.

Alvina remains in high spirits despite the difficult weather in East Africa.

3

A return visit to Kenya

Eight months later I was back in Kenya for another 30-day safari for bongo. I was determined to take one.

This time I had booked a hunt with a different outfitter. Glen was busy and I felt I couldn't wait.

I selected Mike Horsley to serve as my outfitter. It was a wise choice. A blue-eyed, blond young man, he had been highly recommended to me as an outstanding hunter.

Mike was born in England and migrated to Kenya when he was in his teens. He quickly adapted himself to the country, married a lovely English girl named Margaret from Nairobi and bought himself a farm on the foothill of Mount Kenya near the small town of Nanyuki. They had four nice children — three girls and a boy. When Mike was on safari, Margaret ran the farm.

This land was located across the road from the local game warden, Bill Winter. One of the finest and most interesting men I have ever met, Bill is an unusual combination of men. He is a sensitive, kind gentleman, yet he could get as rough and tough as any situation demanded. He, too, came from England at an early age. He entered the Game Department, and because of his resourcefulness and ability, advanced at a rapid pace. While

Preceding pages: Glen Cottar and Pissy rest under the tusk of an elephant, the result of a successful hunt.
Opposite: A group of Masai warriors attired in their beads and robes.

49

still a very young man, he was given one of the most demanding warden jobs in Kenya, the Nanyuki District.

It was more difficult than other districts in Kenya because the constant clearing of land had turned former feeding places of the elephant and buffalo into small farms or "shambas." There were very few days when Bill did not have to take his double rifle in hand and sally forth to defend the settler of the newly plowed ground from some beast that threatened his home or crop. The man could tell wonderful stories by the hour of defending the people and land from the animals of the forest. He married a lovely dark-haired girl named Barbara and they have four children — three girls and a boy.

Both of my other hunts for bongo were on Mount Kenya, but this time we were going to hunt the Abadere Range of mountains about 50 miles north of Mount Kenya. This range of mountains cannot compare with the grandeur of Mount Kenya that rises to a height of over 15,000 feet, topped by jagged peaks of eternal snow. Yet the jungle on the slopes of the Abaderes is just as dense and, while not as steep as Kenya, just as dangerous to hunt. Many times in the next 15 days we were to run for our lives to escape the charges of the stupid rhino that were even more plentiful than on Mount Kenya.

The Land Rover, followed by the loaded lorry, wound its way up the twisting road to an elevation of 8,000 feet. It passed through a small village of Kikuyus, the local tribe that lived in the area. We continued on for five miles when the road came to an abrupt end. We set up camp while several Colibus monkeys watched with great interest. It was dark before the boys finished, and the evening chill that always comes with sundown in the mountains was upon us.

We had hoped for rain during the hunt, but it did not come. Each day was just like the one before. Rising early in the chill of the morning for a quick breakfast, we would plunge into the dense jungle in search of tracks. Or we would climb to the higher ridges, silently working our way along while scanning the opposite side of the canyon for the sorrel red color of the elusive bongo. One morning we were going along a ridge when Mike's gun boy, Medivi, stopped abruptly and silently extended his arm toward a spot in the dense bush across from us. We all stopped and stared at a bright spot of reddish color in a clump of brush.

"Bongo!" Medivi whispered.

I stared at the spot of red, then quickly put my binoculars that always hung around my neck to my eyes. The red spot jumped out at me from the bushes. I could also see ten stripes of white. We were looking at the side of a bongo standing in the bushes. Then the spot moved and a neck and head appeared, decorated by big ears and beautiful lyre-shaped horns.

"Bele?" Mike whispered. "Manimoke," Medivi answered. "It is a female," Mike said, "but a nice one. Will you take her?"

What a decision. The female bongo is one of the very few animals that a sportsman can take in good conscience. The other two are the big female leopard and the female oryx whose horns are quite often longer than those of the male. Female bongo horns grow as long as the male but are much thinner.

I had now hunted bongo for over 30 days and this was the first one I had ever seen. My recollection of aching muscles, tired legs and stinging nettles was very strong at the moment and urged me to take her.

I rested my rifle over a nearby stump, found the shoulder of the beautiful female in the scope and looked at her, now standing completely in the open, nibbling daintily at the tip of leaves on a bush with her neck outstretched.

I hesitated and was lost. The early training to protect the female overcame me. I lowered the rifle. I could not shoot her. I did not know about Medivi and the other boy with us, but I am sure that Mike agreed with me. As the moment passed and the bongo disappeared into the bush, he turned to me.

"Well done," he said. "We will find you a good male bongo."

We waited and watched for awhile, but she was alone. Twice she moved into the open, then was finally swallowed up for good by the jungle. We resumed our careful way, hoping we would see another spot of red or another movement of the bush.

But we did not see another bongo, and the days sped by. Sometimes I almost regretted my chivalrous act until I reminded myself there were only a few bongo left. I would not only have killed one bongo but all her potential offspring. If I could only have seen the spot of red and killed her, I wouldn't have felt too badly. Yet knowing it was a female, I am still glad I did not take her.

On the fifteenth day of hunting we had taken the Land Rover and driven away from the camp to another part of the range where we searched all day without seeing anything. When we returned to the Land Rover, tired and

Not more than 30 yards away, with his great head lowered, was the biggest buffalo I had ever seen.

discouraged, Mike turned to me and said:

"Mac, I think we should end this bongo hunt. It's too dry to track, and we have very little chance of seeing another bongo in this thick bush. I feel like I am taking your money for nothing."

It was a long speech for Mike and I knew he meant it.

"My schedule is set up for a 30-day hunt," I told him.

"Well, let's go down on the Athi River and see if we can kill a big elephant," he suggested.

I shrugged, "OK, if you think that best." We were both rather quiet on the way back to camp. Then suddenly he said, "How would you like to kill a good bushbuck?" "I already have two now," I answered, not too interested. "I mean record book size," he persisted. "Well, that's different.

I am always interested in a book animal."

"I know a small glade right off the road near here where some really big bushbuck feed late in the afternoon. We'll go by and check." A short time later he stopped and cut the motor. I started to get out and he said, "Let Medivi go look and see if any bushbuck are feeding." Medivi got out of the car and sauntered over to a line of bush that bordered the glade. He peeked through the bushes, jerked his head back and motioned for me. I got out of the car, taking my .300 Weatherby with me, and jacked a shell into the chamber ready to shoot the bushbuck. Mike also got out and walked alongside me to where Medivi stood.

When we reached his side I leaned out and looked into the open glade. Not more than 30 yards away, with his great head lowered, staring intently at me, was the biggest buffalo I had ever seen. It was a snap decision. I knew I was under-gunned, but I raised the .300, swung it onto his chest just under the lowered head, and pulled the trigger. He whirled and ran for the thick bush. I hit him two more times before he reached it. He collapsed with the sound of the third shot still ringing in my ears.

We walked over to where he lay in a huge black pile. Mike remarked "You probably didn't realize how good that buff is. He is at least 50 inches." It was getting dark so we left him where he was and went back to the Land Rover. We would tell the villagers about the meat and bring some of them back with us when we took the horns and cape. He was big — 50½ inches on spread, 48 inches on longest horn (5th best ever recorded) and a 16½ inch base, the largest on record at that time. Some of the best trophies are taken through sheer accident.

We left the Abaderes and went back to Mike's house to outfit for the elephant hunt. We also had to get permission from the Game Department to hunt in certain blocks along the river that produced big elephant. On short notice such permission was sometimes hard to obtain. While Mike got the supplies and equipment together, Margaret spent the time calling the Game Department. I visited with Bill Winter who invited me to go on control work with him and his scouts.

I gladly accepted, but when I told Mike about it, he was not as happy. "That Bill will get you killed," he growled. "That is a very dangerous business even for a professional. You know I am responsible for your safety." I insisted on going and Mike decided that he would accompany us. He had done a lot of control work and had killed over 700 buffalo and elephant for the Game Department. The next morning we both reported for control duty at Bill Winter's house.

We set out for the village that had complained about the elephants with two Land Rovers full of men. Mike, Bill and I were joined by several game scouts. We went up the south side of the Abaderes where the Kikuyus had cleared off the jungle to farm small "shambas." This movement to the Abaderes had spread quickly since "uhuhu," the end of the British rule in Kenya. In eight short years the thickly wooded slopes of the Abaderes had been divided into small patches of cultivated earth. Man's encroachment on animals' domain was clearly evident.

Of course, this caused problems. For centuries the buffalo and elephant had fed on the browse and grass where the farmer now planted his maize

A native family comes to collect the meat following the downing of a cape buffalo.

and melons. The urge to visit the area was strong in the animals. Quite often the herds would move back into the cultivated plots and eat the crops. The native could do very little toward defending himself. Most of the time he could drive buffalo out, but more often they grazed at night. The native was not too happy to stay out all night.

The elephant was a different matter. Most of the time the damage was done by families of cows, calves and young bulls. The cows were naturally belligerent. After being driven out of the shambas a few times, they became even more so and were very dangerous. Quite often a farmer was killed while trying to drive a herd of elephants out of his shambas. The people had complained and Bill Winter and his staff had come to the rescue.

We stopped at a small village on top of a ridge where thick jungle had grown a short time before. People came out of small huts and gathered around the Land Rovers. The Kikuyus were a short, stout tribe of Negroes with cheerful, friendly dispositions. The children peered at us from all sides while Bill and his sergeant talked with the men who gestured toward the thick bamboo tangle about a mile from the village. When they concluded, Bill came over to our car. He grinned at me and said, "Well, Bwana, are you ready to shoot an elephant?" "I guess so," I answered and stepped out of the Land Rover, taking my .458 from the man who sat in the back seat.

We started off with two young men from the village leading the way. Bill walked alongside of me with instructions on what to do, "I have a personal forest permit for one elephant," he said, "since we will have to kill one or two to drive them out of the area, we may as well take the best bull we see. You wait until I give you the word." I nodded in agreement and we continued at a fast walk.

We were followed by about half the population of the village but kept losing people as we continued. By the time we entered the bamboo there were only about six young men with us. When the bamboo closed about us, we were in a different world — a dangerous one — because these elephants had lost their fear of man. Ordinarily man-scent is enough to send them in flight through the forest, or it will cause them to quietly slip away. After being harried by the villagers with rocks and sticks until they learned they could not harm them, these elephants would ignore man-scent and when molested, charged.

There was no more talking. We walked along briskly, looking through the open patches in the bamboo for the sight of huge brown or grey bodies.

Then we stopped. Straight ahead the bamboo moved and a young elephant walked out. He disappeared almost instantly back into the bamboo. It was mid-day and the elephants were not moving about very much. Only the youngsters stirred at this time of day. It was hot with no wind at all.

Bill took the lead and moved forward slowly, circling the clump of bamboo where we had seen the young elephant. Then we were among them. Elephants were on all sides of us, their big greyish brown bodies standing perfectly still or swaying gently from side to side. Occasionally a series of bubbling sounds would break the silence as the huge bellies, loaded with fermenting greens, would dispel the gas in gut rumblings.

We looked at several without disturbing them. Then Bill singled out a bull with about three feet of ivory sticking out of his head. "Shoot that one," he directed me.

We were about 25 yards from the bull when I raised the .458, lined up on a spot between ear and eye, and squeezed off. The bull rocked on his feet as the jungle exploded with noise and activity. I still had the gun to my shoulder when, out of the corner of my right eye, another bull stepped out within five yards. Without thinking, I whirled and shot him in the head. Another gun boomed alongside me. Screams of angry and frightened elephants became a frenzy. There were shots being fired all around me. Bill bolted forward after an elephant wounded by some other bullet. I followed, as did the others. When the elephant went down we found ourselves in a small clearing filled with ten female and young elephants. They screamed and moved forward. Bill said something in Swahili that I didn't understand, but one of the scouts flicked a match, set fire to a cherry bomb and tossed it toward the herd.

It exploded with a tremendous noise. Several more bombs were tossed at the herd. The screaming and trumpeting was deafening. The dirt churned as huge, brown bodies flashed by our small party. Only five of us remained; the others had taken flight. The herd faded into the bamboo at a fast trot and headed up toward higher elevation, leaving the clearing to us. I heaved a sigh of relief. I had never been so close to so many elephants. Bill looked around and commented, "Just our party left. Let's 'figger' out who shot what."

Then he turned to me and said, "When I say shoot elephant, I mean one elephant, Bwana." "I'm sorry, Bill," I apologized, "but he was so close to me, it was just a reaction." "No sweat," he replied. "We came here to shoot some and scare the others, and I think we bloody well succeeded. They won't be back for a long time. That's the only way to do it. What did you shoot, Mike?"

"I put two into the second bull Mac shot," Mike said, a little sour, I thought, "just to make sure." A consultation among the scouts and Bill determined there should be four dead elephants somewhere in the bamboo. Sure enough, a search revealed four bodies scattered over a 200-yard area. No wounded elephant had gotten away. I was grateful to Mike for shooting the second bull. A quick examination revealed that my bullet had missed the brain. Both of Mike's shots in the shoulder, about four inches apart, had done the job. By now some of the villagers arrived with huge baskets and knives. Soon the bloody mess of carving tons of meat from the bone and carrying it to the village would begin.

I am glad we left. I had no stomach to see men crawl inside the bloody cavities of the huge animals to hack out the delicacies of heart, liver and fat from the intestines, then pass them through openings in the huge bellies. The sight seen once is usually enough.

We made our way back to the nearly deserted village and our Land Rovers, leaving two scouts to collect the ivory. As I passed Bill and Mike, Bill slapped me on the back and said, "Well done, Bwana. We'll make a control warden out of you yet. You stood fast and firm."

As we walked on to our car Mike commented, "He'll make a control man out of you alright, but you might bloody well get killed before you learn." He started the motor and backed away so Bill could get by.

The day had probably been the most exciting one of my life. I could see where a man could get addicted to the life of a game warden. Bill thoroughly enjoyed the danger and excitement of the job; it was the spice of his life. In later years I went on buffalo control work with him using dogs to bay the animals. It was even more dangerous than elephant control. When the dogs bay a big bull buffalo, it was really something to see.

With 2000 pounds of controlled fury he would charge the dogs, often breaking their backs with his hoofs. At other times he would toss the dogs over his head ten yards away with his long black horns. When tired, he would stand foaming at the mouth with lowered head. Get ready, for one look from his little red-rimmed, hate-filled eyes and he will charge over anything to get to you. It is a very dangerous game.

One day later we were on our way down to Block 29, located on the Athi

The end of a successful chase for a bull elephant.

River. We passed through Nairobi without stopping and took the road leading to Dar Es Salaam. It is a long day's drive from Nanyuki to the Athi River. We arrived at our camping place near sundown after passing through several miles of crisp, brown bush shriveled by the hot, dry wind. There had been no rain in four months. All water, except in the major rivers had dried up.

There were very few species in the area compared to those found in the rich grasslands of the Narok and Kiajaro regions not more than 150 miles away. There were some lesser kudu, giraffe and oribi, but the land was alive with rhino. Yet the big herd of elephants that gather in the dry season was the chief reason we had come.

We pitched our camp a short distance from the river and had dinner,

The land of Kenya was alive with game, including the stately giraffe.

serenaded by jackals and a hungry hyena that prowled nearby. It was a welcome change after the cold, silent nights in the Abaderes.

The next morning Mike drove the Land Rover over to a huge rock that jutted to a height of 50 feet above the ground. I was surprised to see such a rock, but in a few minutes I understood why Mike drove to it. We climbed to the top and walked to the center. From this high point we could see several miles in all directions, including the distant Tsvaso Park.

There were elephants everywhere. Some stood alone; others formed small groups. Mike and I began sweeping the area with our binoculars. We saw several bulls with 60 to 80-pound tusks, but we were looking for a 100 pounder. After four hours of searching, we came off the rock and took the Land Rover through the bush. Two boys sat on the roof of the Land Rover looking over the tops of the bushes for game. It sure was different from most of the elephant hunting I had done in the Tana River country where we looked for tracks, then followed the animal for many miles to get a look at him. We covered a lot of ground and saw many elephants, but none to our liking.

For five days we followed the same pattern — two or three hours of glassing from the rock and the remaining hours spent in driving and looking.

It was on one of these days that we had an incident with a rhino. It was near sundown and we were moving slowly through the bush when one of the boys tapped on the top of the car. "Dorfler," he said, speaking his word for elephant.

We stopped as Mike raised his head through the roof hatch of the Land Rover and glassed the animal. "He is quite a ways off and looks good," he said. "We will have to hurry."

I got out of the car with my .458 in my hand, ready to go. Mike took his .458 and we set off at a fast clip through the bush. The tracker led, followed by Mike, myself and Medivi. We were almost running through the bush.

I have found that most of the time a person gets careless and into trouble when in a hurry. This was no exception. We were proceeding single file, intent on the elephant ahead, when suddenly I was almost knocked down by the two men backing up in front of me. I stumbled to one side just in time to see the huge, black figure of a rhino rise to his feet and swing around to face us not more than 10 feet away.

"Don't run," Mike whispered urgently. "Back slowly." That's all I could do because Medivi had me by the right arm, tugging on it.

The rhino snorted and tossed his head two or three times, then came toward us with short, mincing steps. I shook Medivi loose from my arm and raised my rifle, centering on the rhino's head. I knew to run would be fatal.

"Don't shoot yet," Mike said in a loud whisper. "Don't shoot until I tell you." His gun was also on the rhino who gave every indication that he was going to come on any second.

Then Mike's gun roared. Dirt and gravel flew up and hit the rhino in the face. He stopped, snorted, then turned and plowed off through the bushes. "The stupid bloody bastard!" Mike swore, with relief in his voice. "We would have had bad trouble if we had killed him."

Our elephant stalk was over as we turned around and made our way to the Land Rover. I had learned another lesson. Never hurry through bush in Africa. You never can tell what you may step on. In this case, it was like stepping on a case of dynamite.

Early in the morning of the sixth day we were again seated on top of the rock glassing when Medivi called our attention to five elephants over the boundary in the park.

"Five bulls," he said to Mike. I swung my glasses to check them out. The first bull had what we called "toothpicks," about 25 or 30 pounds of ivory on each side. The second was no better, and the third had one broken tusk. The fourth had his head buried as he ate behind a big bush. The fifth was not too bad; he had about five feet of ivory, but it was very thin.

"The last one to the right looks pretty good," I said to Mike. He, too, had been looking at them.

"They are too thin," he answered, " ... about 80 to 85 pounds, I reckon."

At that moment the elephant smallest in body size stepped away from the bush he was eating. "I'll take that one," I said quickly. His tusks stuck out of his head like two giant pinchers, over five feet in the clear and very thick.

The horns on this cape buffalo measured a full 50½ inches.

The tribes must still resort to primitive ways to complete their work, such as paddling the river in dugouts and carrying firewood on their heads.

It was my first look at really big ivory. No one had to tell me that I was looking at better than a 100 pounder.

"He will go over a 100," Mike said, "but you may not get a chance to take him. He is still in the park on the other side of the nullah."

So he was, but only a few feet from it and grazing in our direction.

There are times in your life when you are strangely confident that things are going your way. This was one of those times. I felt confident that the bulls would cross over the nullah and into open shooting area. On they came, moving slowly from bush to bush, tearing off great bunches of leaves and limbs with their trunks and stuffing them into their mouths.

In a few minutes, while Mike and I kept our glasses glued to our eyes and Medivi and the other man chatted like monkeys behind us, they came into

the dry nullah. The first elephant disappeared into it and emerged on our side, the second followed and the others came along in a steady walk.

"Let's go get him," I said, dropping my binoculars free on my neck and standing up.

"Don't be so impatient," Mike growled. "I want them to get clear of the park by at least a hundred yards."

"Why?" I asked. "They may go back in if we wait too long!"

"We need that much space," Mike answered. "If you don't drop him cold with your first shot he will run for the park."

"You have to be kidding. You don't really believe they know where the park boundary is, do you?"

"As well as you do," Mike answered with conviction. "He will go straight for the park."

We waited as the sweat started to run, both from the hot sun beating on the rock and from the anxiety of the situation. Seldom does one see a 100-pound elephant within shooting range and not be able to shoot him.

When they were at least 100 yards from the dry nullah, Mike stood up. "Let's go get him," he said.

We came off the big rock in a hurry and climbed into the Land Rover. Mike picked up some loose dirt and let it fall free from his hand to test the wind. The wind was good, blowing from the elephants toward us.

We drove quickly through the bush, stopping about a quarter of a mile from where they were feeding.

Mike climbed out with his .458 while Medivi gave me mine. We went through the bush in a fast walk. Time was very important. Without warning the elephants could turn back and be in the park within minutes.

It was no problem in deciding which one was the big bull. The closer we came to him, the better he looked. He was grazing as he walked along parallel to the nullah, almost as fast as a man could walk.

We came within 30 yards of him. Without hesitating for more than a second, I fired into his head, aiming for that small vital spot between his eye and ear. Apparently I missed the brain because after one stunned second, he whirled to follow the other four bulls into the nullah and the safety of the park.

"Hit him again!" Mike shouted. I ran after the bull and emptied my rifle into him. The other bulls left him behind as they raced into the nullah, out again, and in the park.

The big bull staggered on, but while I reloaded, he collapsed in a cloud of dust about 20 feet from the nullah. I thought my heart would jump out of my chest in the excitement of the chase and the thought of losing him in the park. But he was down and feebly kicking in the dirt. Mike walked up and fired in the back of the head. He stepped away, pulled out a handkerchief and mopped his forehead.

"Now, do you believe they know where the park boundary is?" he demanded.

I didn't answer him. It was obvious these bulls knew. I was just thrilled at the sight of the massive tusks that stuck out of his head. If he had crossed over the boundary, I would have lost the ivory. Taking my tape out of my pocket, I circled the top tusk at the lip. The tape read 22-5/8 inches. The other tusk measured 22½ inches — a beautiful set of ivory.

The four of us discussed the probable weight of the largest tusk. Guesses ranged from the skinner's 140 pounds to my 110 pounds. Mike's estimate was closest at 120 pounds. Two days later we weighed them. The largest weighed 121 pounds and the other 110 pounds. Three months later when I received them in California, I weighed them again. They weighed 118 and 108 pounds.

And so another bongo hunt ended without a bongo, although I could have taken a female. Perhaps the gods repaid me for not taking her by giving me the combined best elephant and buffalo in Africa that year. I was awarded the Air France trophy for the achievement.

4

The elusive bongo of Kenya

This time the hunt was for bongo, one of the most elusive and sought after animals of the dense forests of Africa. There are two species. The eastern species is found in the Abadere and Mau Ranges of Kenya and in the dense jungles of Mount Kenya. A few have been taken in the Sudan.

The western species lives in the Cameroons, Central African Republic and the Congo. It is reported that some have been seen in Gabon. Without a doubt, the bongo is the top trophy animal in Africa. Most of these animals have been taken only after much hard work and effort on the part of both the professional hunter and client. However, some bongo have been taken by sheer luck as in the case of a friend of mine on his first hunt to Africa.

He wanted a big buffalo, and one of the best places to take one is on the slopes of Mount Kenya. So he and his professional white hunter set up a camp on Kenya and went looking for a big old bull. Early the second morning they were skirting an open glade, when a big bull bongo stepped out of the forest into the open. The white hunter grabbed the arm of my friend and said, "Shoot, shoot!"

"But that's not a buffalo," my friend answered.

Preceding pages: Beautiful umbrella trees, typical of those found throughout Africa, surround camp Newu in Kenya. Opposite: We began in Kenya after bongo, but settle for an island situtunga in Uganda.

"My God, shoot, that's a bongo," the professional hunter urged.

My friend shot and killed the bongo without realizing the prize he had stumbled on. Such is the luck of the hunt. However, these lucky incidents rarely happen to a hunter more than once or twice in a lifetime. When a hunter has a fine collection of rare and record book animals, most of the time he has had to earn them the hard way, by work and perseverance.

Again my professional hunter for this safari was Glen Cottar. We had developed a friendship that was to last through the years. I consider him one of the best professional hunters in all Africa and now, ten years later, I have not changed my opinion.

It was raining when we left Nairobi and drove the 120 miles to Nyere. We were going to hunt the east side of Mount Kenya. Glen wanted to check certain boundaries with Billy Woodly, the National Park game warden of that area, who was a friend of his.

We stopped at the Woodly home and found that Billy was out working. We waited until he returned about 5 o'clock with some of his park rangers. They had been out on patrol.

Glen explained that we wanted to hunt bongo near the park boundary and asked Billy for a map so we would not wander into the park. Billy said that he would do better than that. He would send a ranger with us. He didn't want to take a chance of us getting into the forbidden area. Billy Woodly is like many of the other dedicated wardens of the Park and Game Departments of Kenya. They take great pride in their work and are responsible for developing the best departments in all of East Africa.

We left Billy's house after dark and started up the muddy, slippery road toward the top of Mount Kenya; it was still raining.

The Land Rover, with its 4-wheel drive and chains on all tires, handled the road pretty well, but the heavily loaded lorry really had a tough time. It frequently slid off the road into the soft mud of the shoulder. When this happened, Glen hooked the Land Rover to the bumper and, with all the boys pushing, we would get her back on the road. On two occasions I also got out and helped push.

We arrived at our camping place at 2 A.M. The boys put up the tents in the rain. It was almost 4 A.M. before we got into bed. It had been a cold, miserable drive.

The next morning the sun was shining and things looked a little better. The men were a bit glum and unhappy, but I could understand that.

Hunting the mountains in Kenya is always hard on the crew. It is always cold at night, and obtaining water is usually a problem. The mountain forest can be depressing to the average person. There is very little to see, and when it rains the mud makes the situation even worse.

Hunting bongo should be done in the rainy season if you want to succeed. This exceptionally wary animal is so spooky that it is almost impossible to come up to him in the dry season. When disturbed by the slightest noise, he is up and away and will not stop for miles.

There are two successful methods used in hunting bongo. One way is to find a salt lick where the animals gather, build a blind in a tree and sit there night and day until a bongo comes to the lick. The other method is much tougher, but more successful. However, it must be done during the rainy season. This was the method we planned to use.

Each morning after the night rainfall, we would follow the elephant trails along the ridges. Or we would walk the other game trails along the mountain streams, looking for fresh bongo tracks. If we did not find fresh spoor by two in the afternoon, we would return to the camp. The reason we did not start on a trail after two, was because we would not have enough daylight left to go very far. We found it usually required from five to seven hours to trail a bongo until he would bed down in the thick bush or bamboo.

Even if you manage to trail one of these magnificent animals to the spot where he decides to sleep, it does not mean that you will bag him. The spot he will select will be the most dense thicket he can find. And if you manage to get within 20 or 30 yards of him by carefully stepping in the footprints of the guide in front of you, you still may not be able to see this animal. He blends perfectly with the thick foliage and bamboo he selects for a resting place. Several times I have had the native guide drop to his knee in front of me and point at a dense thicket. I would stare at the spot and see nothing.

I would raise and lower my head and weave from side to side trying vainly to see what the guide saw.

Then there would be a grunt, a rustle of brush in the thicket and then silence. The bongo had vanished.

When this happens to a hunter, there is a terrible letdown feeling. For miles you have been under pressure, coupled with the supreme excitement of being within a few yards of the animal you are seeking. Suddenly he vanishes. A numbness descends upon you when you think of the long trek

At right, a native tends his flocks along the Tana River. Below, our camp was also located near the same river which flows through Kenya.

back to the camp. You must push your way back through the thick brush, fording the swift mountain streams that you had crossed in search of your quarry. Sometimes the return trip is made in a downpour as the night rains begin late in the afternoon.

For fifteen days Glen and I hunted on the slopes of Mount Kenya. Most of the time was spent in the rain. Then fate decreed that the bongo hunt would come to an end before our thirty days were up.

We drove down the ridge on which we were camped and over across to another. The Land Rover followed an old abandoned trail far above the campsite. We left the vehicle with the driver. Together with two boys, the local man and Pissy, we started climbing higher up the mountain. Our hope was to reach an overhanging peak where we could sit and glass into the open glades below.

We stayed on the outcrop of rock until sundown, looking into the glades and a small swamp where new bamboo shoots were beginning to grow. We saw some very nice bushbuck, a few buffalo and one giant forest hog that was rooting at the edge of the swamp. I wanted very much to shoot the giant forest hog as I had not bagged one, but was overruled by Glen who said it would ruin the spot for further bongo hunting.

The clouds came in on schedule around 5 P.M., and a light rain started to fall. We came off the rock and hurried down to where we had left the Land Rover, arriving at the spot after sundown. We climbed into the Land Rover, Glen turned on the headlights and we started down the ridge.

The trail was not so rough, but in several places small springs had caused soft spots in the trail. Glen almost got bogged down in a few places where the water trickled out of the ground. Only by maneuvering around the bad spots were we able to keep going. With the rain coming down harder in the darkness it was much more difficult to see these soft spots. Twice we were stuck during the first 300 yards, and both times the three boys managed to push us out. Then we hit another hidden spring and were stuck again. This time the three boys could not get us going, even after they had cut limbs from nearby bushes and placed them in front of the wheels. The rain came down harder and the men were soaking wet. I felt sorry for them, and the prospect of staying on the side of the mountain all night didn't appeal to me.

I opened the car door and stepped out into the rain. "What are you going to do?" Glen asked.

"I am going to give them a hand," I said.

There was no objection. However, he later said that was the first time a client, paying $175 a day for a safari, offered to get out and push a vehicle in the rain and mud.

With the 25 percent added manpower, we again got the Land Rover moving. But on one of the violent shoves, I felt a pain in my left side. I forgot the pain after we made it down the ridge and into camp where we enjoyed a hot dinner before turning in.

The next morning the pain in my groin had worsened, and I couldn't go hunting. Two days later found me in Nairobi's Queen Elizabeth Hospital where I underwent surgery. I was hospitalized for ten days before being released with the warning to be careful if I returned to the safari.

Two days before I was released from the hospital, Glen had driven down to the Loiter Hills on the Tanganyika border with our equipment and made camp. I chartered a small aircraft belonging to Jackie Blacklaws (who later died of Sleeping Sickness) and flew down to join Glen. As the bush pilots do in Alaska, Jackie set the light plane down in a small area which the boys had cleared by hand.

It was good to get back into the bush. The Loiter Hills were covered with game. On the way from the airplane to camp, we passed herds of zebra, impala, wildebeest, Grant's gazelle and many more species of small game. Vultures hung in the blue cloudless sky. Glen remarked lions had been heard both nights since their arrival. So we were not too surprised when a few minutes later the boys tapped on the top of the Land Rover and said, "Simba."

We stopped; Glen and I put binoculars to our eyes to stare in the direction the boys had pointed.

"Male and female," Glen said quickly. "Let's have a look."

He turned the motorcar toward a clump of bushes and moved slowly forward.

He was right. There was a big male with a scraggly mane and a beautiful sleek lioness under the shade of the bushes.

"They have been mating," Glen said when we stopped about 100 yards away from them.

"He also has been fighting," he added. "Look at the gash on his nose."

The old lion's nose showed a deep red scratch that had bled heavily, turning his jaws a dirty scarlet. He looked at us with very unfriendly eyes

The Loiter Hills were covered with herds of game, including Grant's gazelle.

while the lioness gazed at some impala several hundred yards away.

"I don't suppose you would want him, do you?" Glen asked.

I shook my head. "No, he doesn't have much of a mane. But let's move over closer. I would like a close-up picture with my movie camera."

"We won't be able to get much closer," Glen remarked as he edged the car forward. "She won't mind, but he could get very nasty."

We moved forward and the lion got to his feet. Glen turned the car to one side. I stood up in the Land Rover with my head and shoulders out through the top and began filming. We were within 20 yards when a snarl began forming on the lion's mouth. The female suddenly got up and strolled forward a few steps. She stopped just as suddenly on her stomach as the big male moved forward to cover her. It was over in a few seconds; they both moved into the bushes.

"How was that for cooperation?" Glen said chuckling.

"Couldn't be better if you had arranged it," I replied.

We arrived in camp in the early afternoon. I shook hands with Scotch, the cook, Malaffo and the others of the crew, while Glen held a conference with two strangers. Both were older men; one wore the green khaki of the game department.

After they had finished talking, Glen came over to me. "You are in luck," he said. "We already have located a leopard."

He then explained that one of the old men was from the game department, the other was from a Masai manyatta a few miles from our camp. The old man from the manyatta had gone to the game department for help after a marauding leopard had taken up residence near his manyatta. He would prowl around the manyatta at night, which upset the Masai.

Ordinarily a leopard would not have been able to terrorize the manyatta. The warriors of "Moran," as they are called, would have killed the cat. However, in this case, all the young men had gone down to the lowlands for a social gathering and had not returned.

It is not unusual for a group of Moran from a small manyatta to be gone two or three months visiting more populated manyattas. The Masai practice free love for the Moran. He takes full advantage of this privilege by visiting manyattas where there are many single girls.

The Masai in the small manyatta had asked for help. The game department had responded by asking the nearest safari camp to kill the leopard. We were the nearest.

We still had enough daylight left to visit the manyatta. With the old Masai directing us, we left camp and headed into the bush. After two hours of maneuvering between trees and other obstacles, we came to a dense growth of bushes. After a short consultation between the old man, Glen and the two gunboys, each of the three blacks took a panga from behind the seat of the Land Rover and started to clear a path for the vehicle.

The boys hacked at the bushes as the Land Rover inched forward. We were going up a gentle slope when suddenly we came into a clearing on a flat plateau surrounded by heavy timbered hills. As we burst into the open, we were confronted with small children who stood staring at the noisy monster that had come from the jungle. Screaming in fright and excitement, they charged through the bushes toward the manyatta a quarter mile away. Two or three lost the single red garments that the Masai wear but did not stop to pick them up. They continued on, stark naked, through the jungle.

It was a very funny sight. All of us in the Land Rover were laughing. This was the first motorcar the Mtotos had ever seen, according to the old Masai.

We continued on our way to the manyatta, finally coming to a stop in front of the opening in the thorn boma that surrounded the mud and cow manure huts. It was a typical Masai manyatta except it was smaller. It had six huts set in a circle surrounded completely by a wall of thorn bush about 8 feet high. These bushes had been cut and dragged into place to protect the goats and cattle at night from marauding lion and leopard.

An entrance to the manyatta was made each morning by removing some

A gallery of Masai women projects the beauty and mystery of the race. They wear long earrings, heavy arm bracelets and shave their heads.

of the thorn bush to allow the goats and cattle to pass through on their way to the grazing grounds tended by teenage boys.

Through the opening we could see the churned up dirt where the cattle had milled about at night. The ground was littered with old and fresh manure. The stench from the manyatta produced by animals and humans was overpowering. Millions of flies descended upon us. In the summer these manyattas are unpleasant with flies and stench, but in winter they become unbearable when the mud, manure and urine from the cattle becomes a half foot deep. The Masai wade through it many times each day.

The mortality rate for Masai children is one of the highest in the world. I have seen manyattas where 50 percent of the people were blind or partially blind by dreaded trachoma. The disease is spread by the millions of uncontrollable flies found in the filth of each manyatta.

There was not a person in sight when we stopped in front of the manyatta. Only the complete silence greeted us. The manyatta seemed deserted.

Then several heads appeared peeking around the huts and thorn wall. The youngsters could control their curiosity no longer as the chattering of many voices broke the stillness.

The old Masai climbed out of the Land Rover and disappeared into the manyatta. A youngster came out cautiously to inspect the motorcar and the white people who drove it. Without a doubt, these children and some of the grownups had never seen a white person, and soon the Land Rover was completely surrounded with people. The women and old men stared at us and whispered to each other while the children became fascinated with their reflection in the small mirror on each fender.

In the meantime, Glen and the old men were holding a conversation punctuated with many gestures toward a rocky hill not far from the manyatta. The conversation ceased, and Glen came over to me.

"How would you like to go into the goat business?" he asked, smiling.

"I am not too excited about it," I answered, "but I would be interested in shooting a leopard. What about this goat business?"

"The chief elder of the tribe just now offered us the two best goats in the herd if we kill this leopard. They are very disturbed about this cat. He has been prowling about the manyatta each night and taken two or three goats." It was a very long speech for Glen to make.

"I don't think I would be interested in starting a goat herd," I said, "but

I hope this is a big leopard. It sure would be nice if he was a large black one. Ask the old man if he is."

"No use," Glen answered. "He definitely will be big or he wouldn't be so aggressive. The old man would lie about him, anyway. If you wanted a black one, this would be a black one. If you wanted yellow, suddenly he would become very yellow. He just wants the cat killed."

We had an impala in the rear of the Land Rover. Now that the conversation had ended, we ran the motorcar to the bottom of the hill where the leopard had been seen. The boys lifted the bait and dragged it up the hill a few hundred feet to a large tree. They opened the stomach and, while Kettete made a drag with the entrails and stomach around the bottom of the hill, Pissy and one of the Masai hung the impala in the tree. The job of baiting completed, we returned to camp after a very interesting afternoon.

The next morning we went back to the tree to check the bait and found that the leopard had fed on it. He had eaten one quarter down to the bone and a portion of the other.

"He must be a hell of a big cat," Glen remarked, "and also plenty hungry to eat so much."

I sat down on the ground since I was still a little weak after my stay in the hospital. The boys began cutting some small bushes to make a blind under Glen's supervision. The only bush close to the bait tree was a good 70 yards away. The boys began to build our blind around this bush.

I complained that it was too far away from the bait, but Glen pointed out that there was no bush growing nearer to the tree. They finished the blind and we went back to camp.

We returned just before sundown, leaving the Land Rover at the manyatta. We silently climbed up to the small blind and slipped quietly inside. We settled down to wait, feeling quite sure this leopard would not be long in coming back to feed. We had been in the blind about thirty minutes when suddenly two teenage boys, driving a small herd of cows, came around the side of the hill. They passed directly under the baited tree, yelling and whipping the cows to hurry them to the manyatta.

Glen stood up and swore at the boys as they passed.

He sat down again and said disgustedly, "Damn it, I told the old man to keep his people and animals away from this area. It's going to be dark before that cat comes down now," he added.

Glen was right. The sun had set behind the mountain and darkness came on fast. I kept my eye close to the hole in the brush through which I planned to shoot, watching the bait. Sometimes you do not see the leopard before he is in the tree. It grew darker. Then there was movement in the tree, but it was so dark I could not see clearly. I raised my rifle and looked through the scope. Finally I could see the leopard lying on a big limb pawing at the body of the impala that hung from the branch below. While I watched, he set his claws into the body and lifted it up to where he lay.

"Do you see him?" Glen asked.

"Yes," I answered, "but not too well. He is lying there with the bait. Should I try it?"

"No, it's too dark," Glen answered. "I don't want the chance of a wounded leopard in the darkness, especially one this aggressive."

By now it was so dark that I wasn't sure I could place the bullet well so I was a bit relieved when Glen said not to try it.

After a few minutes longer we slipped out of the blind and went back to the Land Rover.

On the way into camp Glen remarked this was one leopard that we would not get. When I asked why, he said that we had only two more days in the hunting block and felt the leopard would chew through the impala's legs tonight and carry it away.

"We will just put up another," I said.

"If he carries this meat away, he won't come back to that tree until he had eaten it."

"That's too bad," I answered. "I sure would like to get a close look at that leopard."

The next morning we arose a little late. While we were having breakfast, Glen sent three of the boys back to see if the bait was still there. We finished our meal and prepared to go hunting as soon as the boys returned with the Land Rover.

The time passed. Soon it was noon and boys had not returned. Glen began to worry. Two o'clock passed and they still were not back. At three they came roaring into camp with a very exciting story to tell.

They had arrived at the bait tree to find the impala gone. They tracked the leopard up the mountain where he had carried the half eaten antelope. It was wedged into a tree high off the ground. It must have been quite a tracking feat because the leopard carried the bait above the ground.

When they found the carcass, one of the boys started climbing the tree to get the impala while the other waited on the ground. He had gotten a few feet off the ground when the leopard appeared among the rocks and started growling at them. The boy came down and both of them retreated a short distance from the tree. The cat watched a few minutes, then went back into the rocks.

After a few minutes, the boys, with more courage than good sense, went back to the tree and started to climb it again. Again the leopard came out of the rocks, and again the boys retreated. The men and animal kept up this battle of nerves until the men won out and took the bait out of the tree. They dragged it down the hill so it would leave a trail of scent, then put it in another tree near the bottom of the hill. They knew that in my weakened condition I could never climb very far up the hill. They then built a blind and hurried back to camp.

"That is a damned aggressive leopard," Glen remarked when the story was finished.

Late that evening we again went to try for the leopard, but this time our strategy was quite different from before. Six of us approached the blind talking loudly. Then while three of us, Glen, Kettete and I, slipped into the blind, the others continued past and circled back down the hill. Glen felt that if the aggressive cat had followed the bait down the hill, he may be near and hear us if we tried to get into the blind any other way.

We silently took our places in the blind. I whispered to Glen, "Why did Kettete remain with us?"

"To butt that cat off our back if things don't go right," he answered.

Kettete's black face split in a wide grin of white teeth as he sat down and placed a razor sharp panga across his lap.

I examined the hole I was to shoot from and found it to be too low for me. I changed places with Glen and he stuffed his soft jungle hat in the large opening while making a very small hole higher in the thick cover so he could watch the bait. He remarked as he did so, "I don't need to see the ground, just the bait."

We settled back to wait while the dark shadows grew longer on the hillside. The sun sank lower, bathing the entire area in a warm glow. The birds started chirping softly and hopping among the thickest section of the bushes, looking for a safe place to spend the night. Then they were silent. The hillside was as still as the half eaten carcass tied on the big limb directly

The Kenyan sun leaves a golden glow over the land and casts an even longer shadow from a galloping giraffe.

in front of us.

I kept my eyes fixed on the bait as I relaxed, my gun beside me, the barrel end level with the hole in the thick screen of bushes.

The silence was broken by the short bark of a baboon. It was followed by the cries of other baboons. Glen touched my knee with his. We both knew that the leopard was moving about.

My breathing became shallow with anticipation as I pictured the beautiful savage cat coming down the hill toward us, moving noiselessly on soft, padded feet.

Off to our left, a startled bird twittered, and I knew that it had been disturbed by the leopard. We were absolutely motionless as I stared at the bait in the tree until my eyes ached. In order to rest them, I turned my gaze down to the ground in front of me and got a tremendous thrill. The big leopard was moving softly in the short grass toward the bait directly in front of us. I touched Glen's knee with mine and slowly lowered my hands toward my rifle.

At my touch, Glen moved and disturbed a small branch of the blind, causing the leaves to rustle. At the sound, the big cat flattened out on the ground and swung his head to stare at the blind. He turned, his belly almost touching the ground in a low crouch, his head extended, his mouth slightly open, as he began to stalk the blind.

From a distance of about 18 feet, I could see the fierce green eyes staring at the leaves and limbs while the long slender fangs showed a startling white against the red of his mouth. When he was about 10 feet away, I centered the crosshairs between his eyes and squeezed the trigger.

The blast from the 300 seemed to rock the blind and Glen exclaimed, "What the hell are you shooting at?"

"I just killed a leopard right in front of us — I hope." I answered more calmly than I felt.

"You mean he was on the ground out front?" he asked.

"He sure was, not 10 feet away," I answered. "Let's go look."

"Sit still," he said. "Let's listen for awhile."

So we sat and strained our ears for any sound of a wounded cat while darkness descended upon us. No sound broke the stillness.

"Let's go," Glen said. We went out the rear of the blind and cautiously moved around the front. Kettete held the panga extended in his right hand. We found the leopard not more than 10 feet away from the blind, lying curled in a heap where the force of the 180 grain silver tip had piled him up.

Glen touched him with his foot, then squatted down to pick up the leopard's head. "Well, I'll be damned," he muttered.

"What's wrong?" I asked.

"Take a look at where you hit him," he said.

I examined the beautiful spotted head. There was not a mark on it.

"Open the mouth," said Glen.

When I unhinged the jaws, it became apparent where the bullet had entered. The two upper front teeth were gone. I pressed the head between both hands and felt where the bullet had smashed the cranium from the front to the back of the head. The bullet lay under the loose skin at the back of the cat's skull. He had died instantly without a mark on him except two broken front teeth.

We shook hands across the dead cat and Glen said, "Well done."

It was completely dark when the other boys arrived, having heard the shot that killed the leopard. We used flashlights to light our way back to the dark and silent manyatta where the thorn bush had been pulled into place, closing off the entrance.

Glen turned on the headlights of the Land Rover as we stretched the big leopard to full length where it could be seen. There was movement within the manyatta; the thorn bush at the entrance was pulled aside and the Masai came out.

They crowded around the beautiful cat talking, laughing and touching the spotted coat. I was tired and did not feel too well, so I sat in the Land Rover. From there I could see the beams of light reflecting off the whites of the Masais' eyes and shining teeth.

Suddenly one started rocking on his feet, nodding his head and chanting. It was quickly taken up by the others and soon all were in motion, rocking, chanting and clapping hands. It was a strange sight and one that I will never forget.

After a while, our boys picked up the leopard and put him into the Land Rover. Glen climbed in and the car started forward. In a few minutes the sound of the chanting and clapping disappeared in the distance. There was only the sound of the motor and the breaking of brush as we passed.

"I guess you think you are hot stuff tonight," Glen remarked, glancing sideways toward me and smiling.

"Well, I will say one thing," I answered. "I can see a leopard which is more than I can say about a certain guy. Of course, tomorrow or the next day you will probably chew me out for doing something wrong."

Glen chuckled as the Land Rover groaned its way toward camp.

Thus ended my second safari to Kenya. I was to hunt this lovely country several times, but I will cover those hunts in a book called "Kenya."

The next morning we broke camp and headed north to Uganda. I wanted a situtunga for my collection and Glen thought the Sese Islands in Lake Victoria off the coast of Uganda would offer our best chance.

This trek carried us some 800 miles through very interesting country. We passed the towns of Chemengel, Kissii, Kisumu and Edoret in Kenya. Then on to Kampala, Entebbe and Masaka on the shore of Lake Victoria. We traveled around this second largest lake in the world and stopped on the west side.

It took us three days to make the trip; the weather alternated from sunny warm days to cloudy with occasional showers. The huge lake was covered by small choppy waves and resembled the Atlantic Ocean. We unpacked the lorry, taking the bare essentials with us. We loaded the big rowboat as high as we dared, then rowed out to the cruiser that we had leased from the Uganda government.

It took several trips to get our gear aboard before we ventured out onto the lake.

The Sese Islands are, beyond a doubt, the least desirable place I have ever hunted. It is probably the only place in the world where I would not care to return. They are a small string of little islands located within Lake Victoria 20 miles from shore. Covered with grass and clumps of bushes, the islands

We pitched our tent on the Sese Islands, but found it was an undesirable place to hunt.

also produce medium size trees along the shores. The most unique factor about these islands are the floating islands they produce. In the bays on the south side of the islands, protected from the prevailing winds, strong, fibrous plants grow in profusion. These are water plants that grow very rapidly in all directions on the top of the surface. They form a mat of roots, leaves and bulbous growth. Even tall grasslike reeds are sometimes a part of this vegetation.

The matted carpet is home for the situtunga, along with the hippo, crocodile and a few water snakes. When hunting on this grass, it is best to carry a long, stout pole. In some places the vegetation is so thin you can break through the surface. A pole can keep you from going under the water which is often 15 to 20 feet deep in the bays.

The situtunga's feet have adapted to walking on these porous floating islands. The hoofs are elongated and split; when the animal takes a step, his foot spreads in a wide vee to support his weight. The crocodiles have no problem because they swim under it, and the hippos simply smash their way through the growth with their great strength.

It is this action of breaking through the vegetation that causes the creation of the floating islands of Lake Victoria. Occasionally the hippos will almost completely sever a large section of vegetation from the main body. Then the wind will change and blow away from the bay, breaking the section completely free. Many times people on boats and large passenger ships will see a greeen island the size of a large building bobbing along on the water.

Yet the most unpleasant thing about the Sese Islands is the mosquitoes. There are millions of them that make life miserable for you at all hours, except in the middle of the day when it is too warm for them. We had two small pup tents for Glen and I and a new dining tent with a mosquito proof screen on one side. Each night when we had dinner in the tent, the screen would get so covered with mosquitoes you could not see through it. The entire screen became a solid 7 x 10 foot wall of insects.

When I went to bed at night, I zippered down the door, then sprayed the inside of the small tent to kill the insects. It was rather difficult to breathe for awhile, but at least I could sleep for the remainder of the night.

We hunted eight days on two of the islands. I killed two fine situtunga, both of them ranking high in the record book. I also shot my first hippo on the second island when we went for firewood. The island had a small village of people who led a difficult life. They must have lived entirely on fish. I don't see how they could have killed the situtunga, and they certainly did not have the equipment to kill a hippo.

I went with the boys to gather firewood the day I took the hippo. Glen

was waiting for a call on the radio and stayed in camp.

We were riding along in the small boat when Pissy called my attention to a hippo eating grass quite a distance from the water.

"Manamoke or Bele?" I asked.

He took my binoculars and studied the animal carefully, "Bele," he said with finality.

After he had announced the animal as a male, he looked at me with a quizzical expression. After all, the paying client does not go hunting a dangerous animal alone.

I grinned at him. "Safari?" I asked. A wide smile split his face as he nodded his head. "Safari, safari," he answered, turning the boat into the shore.

We got out and crept along the bushes toward the hippo. Pissy was testing the wind just as he did for "Bwana" Cotter. He was enjoying himself, and I knew he wanted to see if I could get the job done. It is well known the hippo kills more natives of Africa each year than any other animal except the crocodile.

We kept downwind from the hippo, placing us almost between him and the water, a dangerous place to be.

We kept behind the bushes and walked to within 60 yards of the animal before coming to an open space. Pissy stepped aside and waited, grinning

The Uganda Government rented us a boat so we could travel on Lake Victoria and to the many floating islands.

The back of the boat was the perfect location for drying our hippo meat in the sun and wind.

from ear to ear.

I thought to myself, I'll show this grinning monkey. I'll shoot this animal right through the head and drop him cold.

I stepped out from behind the bush with the hippo broadside to me, lined up the front bead of the .458 Browning on the hippo's head and squeezed off.

I could actually see where the solid passed completely through the head, blood spurting out on both sides. The hippo wobbled, turned and headed for me and the water.

"Shoot, shoot," Pissy was yelling.

Again I lined the heavy rifle on the oncoming hippo and when the sight settled in the center of the high shoulder hump, I again pulled the trigger.

The hippo crashed to the ground. He had cut the 60 yards in half before falling for the last time.

Pissy probably got more kick out of this short safari than anyone. He laughed, did a little jig and shook my hand.

The other boy, Malaffo, came from the boat bringing my cameras. Just like down in the bush country of Somali, within ten minutes a half dozen natives stepped out of the bush with knives and pots in their hands for the meat.

Pissy and some of the boys cut the jawbones out with the ivory intact. Then Pissy cut the loin straps from the back of the animal for our meat before turning the carcass over to the villagers who had increased to about thirty in number. I have never seen a more hungry look on faces than the group that surrounded the hippo.

We returned to camp after loading the boat with dry wood from the big island. Glen was waiting when we docked and didn't seem too happy.

"Where have you been all this time?" he wanted to know.

"We went hippo hunting," I said.

"In the water?" he asked.

"No, out on land," I answered.

"That is very dangerous," Glen said. "You are not supposed to hunt alone, you know that."

"Well, it seemed like a good thing at the time," I answered, "and besides, Pissy encouraged me."

Glen scowled at Pissy. "That Nugu will get you killed if you listen to him."

Two days later I killed my second situtunga. We left the desolate, insect ridden islands for the mainland and home, ending another 45-day safari for me.

5

Back in Kenya for bongo

Once you have started to hunt bongo, the urge to take the animal becomes almost overpowering to the point of madness. The more you try and don't succeed, the stronger the urge becomes.

One year after my first attempt to take this rare and elusive animal, I was back in Kenya for another go at it.

My guide was again Glen Cottar whom I had come to like and respect, not only as a top professional hunter, but also as a good friend. He had married a lovely young girl named Pat from Njoro, Kenya. They had started their family with a beautiful little girl named Tana.

On this trip I was accompanied by another friend, Walter Neilson, a young hunter from Los Angeles. His guide was Owen MacCullum, a friend of Glen's and a man I had come to know quite well from my three prior safaris to Kenya.

Owen was a fine hunter. He was a small man who did not weigh more than 140 pounds, but he possessed the heart and courage of a lion. He was married to a pretty young woman named Lee who was born in Kenya. They had three nice children, two boys and a girl.

Opening pages: A lion and his mate enjoy the warm sun of Kenya.
Opposite: The king of the jungle surveys his territory.

We planned to hunt fifteen days in the Mara River Triangle area southeast of Nairobi, then split up the party. I would hunt bongo on Mount Kenya, and Walter and Owen would go down to Block 66 near the Tanganyikan border close to Mount Kilimanjaro. Fifteen days was about all one could stand in the jungles and mountains of Kenya when hunting bongo. The Mara River Triangle was, without a doubt, one of the finest areas in all of Africa for hunting plains game and the big cats — especially leopards. On this trip we put out seven leopard baits and had six leopards feeding.

Our camp was located on the escarpment overlooking the Mara River. At any time of the day we could see hundreds of animals below us feeding on the green grass along its banks.

Walter was anxious to film the hippo in the river. The first thing he and Owen did was head for the water with a motion picture camera while Glen and I started putting up leopard baits. That evening when we met for "Sundowners," Walter already had his first African incident to tell.

He and Owen had found two hippo out of the water when they got to the river. A bull and a cow stood on a sandbar about ten feet below and ten yards away from the bank on which they were located.

Walter whispered to Owen, "What luck! Two out of the water and very close! We'll get some good pictures," he said enthusiastically.

The little professional hunter nodded and casually leaned the .500 Hollond and Hollond against a tree while Walter set the legs of the camera stand on the ground to adjust the camera level.

"Those hippo didn't pay the slightest attention to us," Walter said, "until I started filming. Through the aperture I could see the ears of the big bull begin to twitch. Then suddenly he turned toward us and came barreling up the bank. He got bigger and bigger until he filled the aperture. There was a deafening 'BANG! BANG!' I stumbled away from the camera, got tangled up and fell down."

He regained his footing in time to see the bull slowly slide back down the bank of the river with blood pouring out of two holes not more than three inches apart in his head. In one fluid motion MacCullum had snatched up his rifle and shot the hippo only a few feet away from Walter and the camera.

"I never thought a big animal could move that fast," Walter said. He hoisted his glass of scotch and looked through it into the fire. "I sure could

Alvina always enjoyed the baby rhinos, such as this one we found in Kenya.

have used this about then," he added.

MacCullum laughed, "You didn't do too bad, Walter. At least you didn't wet your pants. I have seen some who did."

We had fabulous hunting the next ten days, taking all kinds of plains game and two good leopards. Lions were everywhere, roaring all through the night, but I did not see any I wanted. After you kill three lions, you get real particular about shooting them if you are the right kind of hunter.

We had two experiences with them in camp that were interesting.

MacCullum and Walter hung up a zebra for bait, but there was so much game the lions ignored the zebra for three days. Then one night at dinner we heard roaring from where the bait hung.

"Let's go down and have a look," Glen said. Everyone agreed. We got

I traveled to Botswana in order to take this fine Eastern roan.

into his open Land Rover and pushed off in the direction of the sound.

As we came up to the lone tree that stood in an open field, lions walked off in all directions. A lioness, standing on her hind legs tearing at the bait, was the last to leave the glare from the headlights. She growled fiercely on her departure. The zebra hung by its hind legs in shreds about seven feet above the ground.

"Let's turn off the lights and see what happens," MacCullum suggested.

Glen switched them off and everything became quiet. Then little noises were heard — the rustle of grass, a small stick breaking and the whisper of huge bodies moving about. I don't know about the others, but I felt quite naked sitting in the open Land Rover with so many lions moving about us.

There was a growl right alongside the Land Rover, and Glen switched on the lights. At the same time MacCullum produced a flashlight and turned the ray on the side of the car. Not three feet away stood a lioness with her mouth partly open and tail switching. She remained for a moment, then walked away toward the bait. Several lions were lying or walking under the swinging zebra.

MacCullum played the flashlight around the Land Rover. Many pairs of eyes reflected the light like twin balls of fire.

"Bloody awful lot of lions here," he remarked casually. "Must be over twenty odd." Glen started the Land Rover and we backed away, leaving the area to the lions. I had had enough of the cats for one night.

However, we were not through with the lions. The following evening they wandered into camp, tripped over the tent stakes and made a nuisance of themselves. The next night I was sleeping soundly when suddenly I was awakened by fierce growling a few feet away. The tent began to shake as big bodies were thrust against the canvas.

I rolled out of bed, at the same time reaching for my rifle and snapping on my flashlight. I felt the fighting lions would be in my tent in another moment.

Then the growls subsided, the tent stopped shaking and all was quiet. I

Professional white hunter Ian Henderson poses with a beautiful red lechwe.

went back to bed but did not sleep for quite some time.

The next morning I met the others for breakfast.

"What happened down at your tent last night?" Glen asked. My tent was the last one in the row. "I don't know," I answered, "but it scared the Hell out of me. I thought the lions were coming into bed with me."

"I don't understand it," Glen said. "They don't usually disturb anyone."

"They wouldn't disturb you anyway," MacCullum said. "Your snoring scares them away." His tent was next to Glen's.

"I may snore, but I don't grind my teeth as though I was eating rocks like you do," retorted Glen.

Just then Malaffo, the truck man, came up to the dining tent, rolling a truck tire. "Bwana, look at what the lions did to the tire," he said in Swahili. Glen picked up the tire and examined it.

"Well, I'll be damned!" he said. "Look at this bloody tire!"

We crowded around to see. Several puncture marks appeared in the rubber when Glen pressed from underneath, the marks opened into deep holes. "They have bloody well bitten right through the tire," MacCullum said.

As we reconstructed the incident, we concluded two lions had grabbed the tire at the same time, and in their struggle to take it from each other, bumped into my tent.

Malaffo admitted he had left the tire behind my tent after taking it off the lorry. So the mystery of the fighting lions was solved; they were playing with the tire.

Two days later, Owen MacCullum came down with a high fever and became very sick. When he left for Nairobi for treatment, Glen and I agreed to let Walter join us for the remainder of the hunt, then we would take him into Nairobi.

Poor Owen never did fully recover. He completed one more hunt but died of cancer within a year. He was a fine, courageous man whom everyone highly regarded.

We hunted two more days, then started back to Nairobi. We had to make camp before reaching the city and would sleep in the open without tents. When the beds were made up during dinner, two were placed close together; the third was taken about fifty yards to the nearest bush. The mosquito nets were draped over the beds and all was ready.

Walter had not said much while the beds were being made, but had carefully watched the entire procedure while we ate.

Finally, when we were sitting around the fire after dinner, he looked over at the bed near the bushes and said:

"Whose bed is that?"

"Yours," Glen answered, without a smile. "I understand that you snore."

"Not that much," Walter answered, shaking his head. "Besides, there may be some more lions or leopards about."

Glen burst out laughing and ordered the messman to bring the bed back with the others. White teeth showed in the wide smiles on the black faces of the boys. They had enjoyed our little joke, too.

After one day in Nairobi, Walter and MacCullum went down to South Kenya while Glen and I went up on Mount Kenya. We decided to hunt the east side of the mountain; however, there was little difference in the terrain. We still had the bamboo and thick bush, but now we had an added nuisance — the stinging nettle.

The plant grows over five feet tall and is completely covered with small needles that cause intense itching and burning when touched. It is impossible to hunt in an area without frequently bumping into the plant. At the end of a day's hunt, your legs and arms feel as though they are on fire.

Bongo hunting is very monotonous, with the same procedure each day — finding tracks and following them. During this hunt the expected rain did not fall and tracking was tough. We spent some time in a machan overlooking a salt marsh but saw no bongo. We spotted a good giant forest hog rooting in the swamp, but we passed him up. The shot would have ruined the area for bongo.

So the days went by without further incident, although we came close to bongo on two occasions. Once the animal smelled us and bolted when we came close to him. Another day we ran out of time while on a fresh trail. Yet this hunt only whetted my appetite to take a bongo. I swore I would come back to hunt him again.

6

The unspoiled land of the Chad

Africa offers no country more interesting to hunt than the Chad. It is one of the largest in Africa and lies near the center of the dark continent. The topography ranges from subtropical in the southern part along the Aouk and Shari Rivers to the hot or cold sands of the dry Sahara Desert that cover over two-thirds of the northern country.

Some of the most beautiful and rare animals of the world live in this country. Up north, the three most beautiful and exotic are the addax, the dama gazelle and the scimitar oryx.

These animals are all large. The dama, weighing about 100 to 130 pounds, is the smallest, while both the scimitar oryx and his cousin the addax, will weigh well over 200 pounds. All three share a unique problem: they may live a lifetime without taking a drink because they exist on the Sahara with little water. It can only be found in small hidden springs that flow from the mountain crevices or in the few oases surrounded by green date palms that dot the desert like shining gems in this dry land.

Where there is water, the humans have taken over with their domestic animals, leaving no room for the wild animals.

How do they live without water? They get enough to survive by eating

Opening pages: A beautiful herd of eland graze in the rolling green plains of the Chad.
Opposite: It was a land that provided some fine addax.

103

grass early in the morning when it is loaded with dew from the clear cold nights.

The digestive system of these desert animals does not demand much liquid. Fresh droppings from an animal are very dry and will crumble to dust with a little pressure from your fingers. The fresh pellets from these animals look and feel like pellets several weeks old from animals that live where there is more water.

Along the large southern rivers, the Shari and Aouk, lives the largest of all antelope in Africa, the giant eland. He is one of the most handsome of all animals with great thick horns. They grow to a length exceeding four feet. A ridge over an inch high curves around the entire length of the horn, ending at the tip. His winter coat of light brown hair — tinged with gray on an old bull — gradually darkens toward the shoulders of the animal. As many as twelve white stripes run from the backbone down to the belly, and a black and white vee on the neck at the shoulders complete this magnificent animal's coat.

There are many more species of animal in the Chad, including the big five. Four of the big five are quite plentiful, but there are not many rhino.

The Chad has been hunted very little by the white man. The country is remote, difficult to get into and lacks professional outfitters. Since the French withdrew from the country, the all-black government has not encouraged safaris to the interior, due to the general unrest among the different tribesmen constantly at war over water rights. During the past few years there have been incidents of violence and death on safaris.

I hunted the Chad in January which is the best possible month to hunt. The rains in the south along the rivers were over, and the muggy heat which begins in April and runs through the summer months was not present. The Sahara Desert is also delightful in January, with warm clear days and sparkling cold nights. In later months, heat on the desert rises to over 130 degrees during the day.

This former French colony is, without a doubt, one of the most interesting and productive of fine trophy class animals in the world. When I hunted there, the country was still primitive and unspoiled; today I am quite sure that many areas remain the same. It will be one of the last African countries to lose its game, because it is remote and a truly difficult area in which to live. Half the country lies in the Sahara Desert, sparsely settled by nomadic people who move constantly.

The southern country is rapidly being populated by agriculturists who become more sophisticated each year, and the game will vanish within a short span of time. But the beautiful scimitar oryx with his long curved horns, the stately dama gazelle and the spiraled horned addax will be around for a long time to come, for their land is a bleak and forbidding country with very little water and temperatures ranging from freezing to 140 degrees.

A very fine man and a good hunting companion, Dr. Edward Chatwell of South Gate, California, was my partner on my safari to the Chad.

Although I prefer to hunt alone, the Sahara Desert requires two vehicles or hunting cars. It is not safe to venture out on this vast expanse of hot sand and rock in one car. Quite a few men have perished when their car stalled. If you have two cars and drivers, you must pay almost double the price of a safari, and cost becomes prohibitive. So I asked Ed to join me, and I am glad I did. He was a fine companion.

We arrived in Fort Archambault and were met by Claude Vasselet and Guy Croc, our two professional hunters. We went straight to a house that Claude owned in the outskirts of the small town. No time was lost in getting started as Claude is a very efficient and capable man. In a matter of two hours, we were on our way to the giant eland found along the Aouk River in the Ubangi area of the Chad.

A camp had been set up prior to our arrival. Ed and I stowed our gear in one of the tents and were ready to go hunting.

This area was quite dry, and most of the game was concentrated near the river where water was available, so we hunted along the banks early in the morning and late in the afternoon near sundown.

There were a few scattered villages with small plots of ground where the natives grew maize, corn and sweet potatoes. I was amazed that all local people spoke French in addition to their native language. Claude explained the French settlers believed in having the natives learn the French language in all their colonies and that no Swahili was spoken at all.

This is in direct contrast with the East African countries settled by the English and the Germans, where Swahili is spoken by most of the tribes as a second language. I missed hearing Swahili as it has always been a part of Africa to me, and I have learned a bit of it.

There were the usual African animals along the river in this area, with the exception of elephant, which I didn't see during the fifteen days we spent hunting there. I heard lions twice at night and saw spoor of both lion and leopard. However, the special animal that I wanted from this area was the Lord Darby eland. He is far superior to the East African and Livingston eland in both length and body size. He can weigh 900 to 1000 pounds.

Other animals that I wanted for my collection from this area were the harness bushbuck and the Northwestern buffalo.

I took both of the two animals without any unusual circumstances, but the giant eland eluded us each time we came on his spoor and tried to track him down.

Something did occur on this trip that has never happened to me before or since. It took place on one of our daily drives along the river.

Several mornings we had seen a herd of hartebeest coming from the river after drinking. There was usually a bunch of cows — some calves and two or three young bulls — but nothing worth shooting.

Then one morning we passed them and saw a big old bull. Claude urged me to take him.

I started to get out of the Rover and Claude said, "He is watching us and

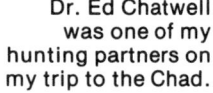
Dr. Ed Chatwell was one of my hunting partners on my trip to the Chad.

will spook the minute you hit the ground. Shoot him from here; he is a good one."

I leaned forward, rested on the windshield frame (the glass was down so we could get air), took careful aim at the bull's shoulder and squeezed off a shot. The bull flinched and shook his head, but didn't run. "What happened?" Claude asked. "He is only about seventy yards away."

"Damned if I know," I answered, still looking through the scope. I jacked another round into the barrel and squeezed off again. The old bull lunged forward about three feet, spun one turn and fell to the ground. We drove up to where he lay, got out and walked over to him.

"I can't understand how you missed him on the first shot," Claude remarked.

"I don't know either," I answered. "Strange things happen sometimes; maybe I flinched."

We both examined the hole in the shoulder where the bullet had entered, then walked back to the Rover while the boys prepared to skin the animal out.

I heard an exclamation from one of them and he called to Claude in French. "Let's go see what he has found," Claude said. We walked back to the hartebeest; the boys had turned him over and were looking at two bullet holes an inch apart.

"You did hit him both times," Claude said. "Look at that."

"That's impossible," I said. "The bullet must have split and made two exits."

"No, you hit him twice, but both bullets went in the same hole and out at different angles." We turned the bull over and looked closely at where they had entered the shoulder. Sure enough, the wound was not quite round, but rather oval-shaped.

Claude shook his head. "I have seen many animals shot," he said, "but never two bullets in the same hole before."

"Why didn't he run?" I asked.

"The Weatherby 300 is a very fast bullet," Claude explained. "We were very close, too. He probably didn't feel it much; perhaps like a fly biting him. He was dead and didn't know it."

We hunted the giant eland hard each day with no luck. It looked like we would fail. We even crossed the river and hunted all day in the Central African Republic to no avail. However, I did see something very interesting while crossing the river. We entered an area where many mud objects dotted the ground. Claude explained these were termite nests built in the shape of mushrooms to provide shade and protection from the heavy rain that sometimes fell. Upon closer observation, I found many openings under the oval-shaped dome and concluded they were for air passage or air conditioning. Who can say that only humans think? Here was a very ingenious structure for this hot country and I, a builder, appreciated it.

A few days later, I finally shot a giant eland after stumbling upon him quite by accident. He was over the book by almost an inch, making me very happy. They are magnificent, huge animals and my quest to find one for my collection had ended. Ed took an eland a few days later that was almost two inches longer than my trophy.

We packed up, departed the Ubangi-Chari area and returned to Fort Archambault. After loading two lorries and a metal trailer pulled by a jeep with fuel, water and supplies, we departed for the northern part of the Chad. The road led into the Sahara Desert, the town of Abache, the oasis called Oom Chalouba and the fort of Fada.

This is savage, forbidden land unless you are properly prepared for it. More than one group of mummified, dried human figures have been found on this hot wasteland. Many more missing hunters have never been located. One mistake is often fatal.

The first day after crossing over the Chari on a pontoon ferry, we found the road that had been laid by the French settlers. We made good time, camping about 175 to 200 miles out of Fort Archambault.

Claude suggested that we stay two days before pushing off into the desert. I am pleased we did because I collected a very good Western roan, Western kob and korin — also known as a red fronted gazelle — before moving on.

It was here that I saw my first column of army ants on the move and was fascinated by what I witnessed. There was a broad line of ants, measuring about two feet wide, advancing in a solid stream over 200 feet long. I could understand how the insects could terrify anyone or anything that lay in their path. The black ants were about one inch long and possessed large manacles that were as sharp as a pair of nippers. I threw a bird that I had shot in front of the advancing hoard and it disappeared immediately under the black wave.

After two days we packed up and drove into Abache, a colorful small town that sits on the edge of the Sahara. It had served as a check out station for desert travelers during the French Occupation of the Chad. If you did not have sufficient water, gasoline, oil and spare parts or if your vehicle was not in good mechanical shape, you were denied entry by the French Foreign Legion.

All that had changed by the time I hunted the Chad. The sentry post was deserted, the wooden gate that once barred the way was broken and there was no one to check your supplies. The feeling of the Chad officials had changed. If the white man wanted to leave his bones on the desert, it was all right with them.

We spent the night at a small inn managed by an old French couple intent on remaining in the Chad until they died. The food was good and the small room was comfortable. However, we were warned to lock our door at night and leave nothing outside or it would disappear by morning. We also found that there were only twelve white people in the total 10,000 living in Abache.

Next morning, we visited the bazaar and found it most colorful. Claude bought some fresh vegetables, some peanuts and other supplies that would last a few days. We loaded the vehicles and started out into the Sahara Desert, a place I had dreamed of visiting since I was a boy.

We immediately hit deep sand within the first fifty miles. The truck and Rovers could not move over the soft surface, as the wheels were buried down to the axles.

Then I was treated to a good example of French ingenuity. Claude had his men unload some long spans of steel mesh treads about 30 inches wide and 15 feet long. These were coupled together and sank very little into the sand even though the trucks were heavily loaded. Four men would pick up each section after the truck passed over it and lay it in front of the vehicle again. It was a slow process, but it worked.

Claude appeared to be worried. When I asked the reason, he said that the bad road would make it impossible to avoid an area where the people were very hostile.

Near sundown, we came to the end of the last sand patch and the land turned to gravel. In the distance, I could see a rocky escarpment. Claude stopped the lead vehicle and we all got out to stretch ourselves.

Ed Chatwell came up with his usual cheerful grin on his face and wanted to know why we had stopped.

"We must camp pretty soon," Claude said. "We cannot move very well on this road in the dark. Do you see those rocks up there?" he asked Ed. Ed nodded his head. "The people who live in a small village at their base are all bandits," Claude said. "They are really bad people. I would like you and Mac to hold your rifles in your hands so they can see we are armed. We will lean some rifles up in the car so they can see we have plenty more."

We followed his instructions and moved up the incline into the small village which consisted of several tents and mud huts. We were met with hostile stares from the dark men and women who possessed Arabic features. Some of the men carried long muzzle loading rifles. They all wore a curved dagger on their belt. It was a very savage and unhospitable group of people.

We were not too many miles out of their village when the sun set, and we were forced to make camp. We did not put up a tent. Supper consisted of cold cuts of meat, bread and some good jam that Claude had brought from Fort Archambault.

After dinner, the men set up a pole ten feet high and placed the four cots around it. A gas pressure lantern was hung about eight feet off the ground. A short distance away, another pole was erected with the men's bedrolls below and a light above. However, there was one difference. Claude's dog, Beady, was allowed to roam in a 40-foot circle around our beds. He had been brought from Fort Archambault and was considered a very good watchdog. Needless to say, a loaded rifle was under each bed.

I went to sleep, lulled by the soft sound of sand as it rustled against my bed, spread by the gentle force of the desert breeze.

We were up at dawn and into the sharp crisp chill of the desert air. A little hot water heated on the kerosene camp stove made coffee and warmed our porridge. Within a short time we were on our way. It was then that Claude told me about two Frenchmen whose heads were found stuck on poles along the side of the road, not far from where we had slept.

I saw my first and only aardvark during the day. A weird, prehistoric creature who has not changed much in thousands of years, he was busy digging a hole in the ground and he did not hear us until we were almost upon him. He came very near to us in order to retreat back into his den. He resembled a huge armadillo, except he did not have a shell on his back.

It was also the day I shot my first dorcus, a lovely, dainty gazelle with ridged horns that curve back, then out, much like his cousin the korin.

We were on the road one more day before we came to the famous oasis of

The fort at Oom Chalouba reminds many of those seen in old Gary Cooper French Foreign Legion movies.

Oom Chalouba. It was a disappointment to me. I had expected to find a beautiful spring flowing from the ground with date trees bordering the water. Colorful Arab tents filled with nomadic tribes would be living in harmony.

What we found was circular well about twelve feet wide, filled with deep, clear water. There were no trees at all in the sun-baked area. People often fought and died in arguments over who would first water their flocks of scrawny, fat-tailed sheep and dirty camels. The fort, unlike the oasis, did not disappoint me. If you have ever seen Gary Cooper in "Beau Geaste," a wonderful French Foreign Legion motion picture, you have seen the fort at Oom Chalouba.

Here all similarity ends. The fort is also dying. What was once a colorful, proud band of men filled with the French esprit de corps that conquered the fierce desert bandits and maintained law and order, had deteriorated into a pitiful, small group of dirty, lackluster men who placed little value in their proud heritage.

Known as the camel corps of the Chad Government, they were trying to keep peace between the two principal groups in the area, the Goran Negro tribe and the Arab Desert people. They often clashed, resulting in several dead men. Not long prior to our arrival, thirty-two men were killed in one confrontation.

The Goran is a warlike race and has one of the strangest ways of proving

manhood. When a boy reaches puberty he must kill another man before he can become a respected man or get married. It does not matter if the victim is young or old, awake or asleep. It simply means the boy must kill a man.

Upon reaching puberty, a boy receives three narrow, serrated spear heads from his father. It is up to the boy how he uses them.

When the French came to the Chad and settled, they were faced with this strange custom. As practical men, they coped with it in the following manner. When a boy reached maturity and killed another man, the French immediately took him into protective custody. They then contacted the tribes of the boy and of his victim. At a conference presided over by the French officer in charge, a settlement was reached on how many camels, sheep or donkeys were to be paid. A young man was considered to be worth more than an elderly man. After an agreement was made, both tribes went their way and warfare was kept at a minimum.

Now that the French have left the country, the tribes are constantly at war with each other.

We left Oom Chalouba with both trucks heavy with supplies. Two fifty-gallon drums were stored on the iron trailer, one with gasoline and the other filled with water, some loaves of bread, our bedrolls, a frying pan and a kettle. We pushed off into the Sahara Desert. Our idea was to be very

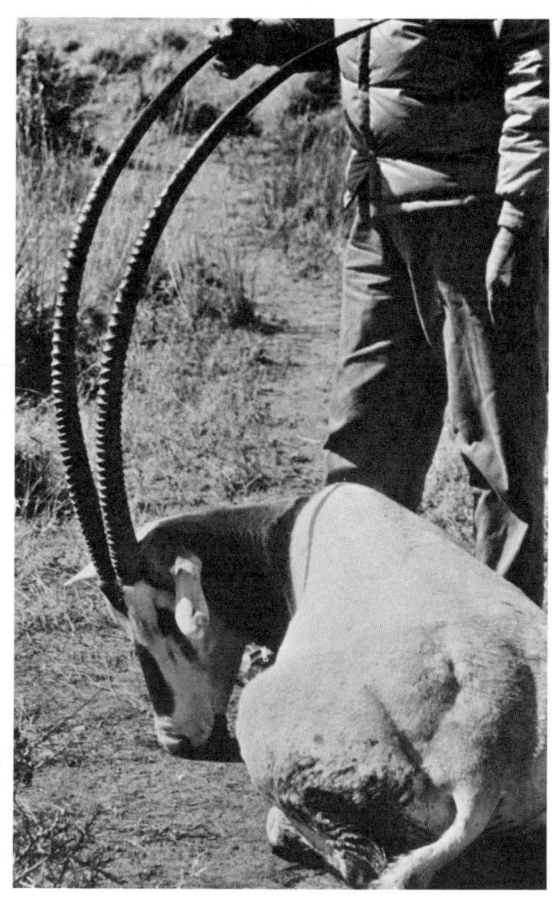

Both Ed Chatwell and I took record book scimitar horned oryx in the Chad.

mobile. We would live off the land and sleep on the sand under the stars.

We headed north toward Fada. Each day I shot a dorcus for our breakfast, lunch and dinner. Within three days we found a great herd of scimitar horned oryx. Ed and I took record book heads. We also took addax and the beautiful, long-necked dama gazelle. Both of my damas and one addax made the book.

It was a very efficient operation, and we covered a lot of ground despite the cold nights. Without the long, heavy tarp that Claude had tied between the two Rovers to break the wind, we would have been very uncomfortable. The desert wind is bitterly cold after sunset.

From the time I was a boy on the farm, I had thought of the Sahara as one vast stretch of sand dunes with no vegetation at all. Now I learned differently. Much of this fascinating desert had sparse vegetation. Sometimes very thick grass pops out of the ground overnight after a hard downpour. Rainfall is rare and comes from six months to two years apart.

When it rains, the grass sprouts like magic, growing six to twelve inches within ten days. It produces seeds and then dies within another three weeks. The seed drops to the ground and reproduces again when it rains, even after two years or longer.

The great herds of scimitar horned oryx and the smaller herds of addax follow the path of the rains. They feed on green and dried grass, staying in an area a month or two, then moving on when the grass is gone to find another swath of grass on the otherwise barren desert.

Both animals, as well as the dorcus and dama gazelle, may live their entire lives without taking a drink of water.

In five days we were back in Oom Chalouba among the groaning camels, bleating sheep and shouting Arabs and Gorans. We came only to refuel and get a few meager supplies before heading northwest to the Ennedi Mountains to hunt barbary sheep.

We followed the tracks of an old army road for a long distance before turning off and going toward a line of low mountains that seemed to rise abruptly out of the sands of the desert. We had come to the Ennedi Mountains, home of the barbary sheep.

We arrived late in the afternoon as the sun's rays colored the surrounding peaks a dark red, and the cliffs and gorges a deep purple — a truly beautiful sight.

Not knowing where to find water when night found us, we pulled the Rovers together, hung up our tarp and laid our beds on the sand. The cry of a jackal was the last sound I heard that night.

The next morning as we drove along the base of the sandstone hills, I was reminded of the peaks in the Zion National Park of Utah, where wind and natural erosion had created unusual designs in the soft sandstone. There were places where the wind had carved a hole right through a mountain peak.

Our guide from Oom Chalouba said there was water along the base of the mountains. We were still looking for it at noon when we came upon an old man riding a donkey. The guide spoke to him and the old man responded by pointing to a distant clump of trees. Fifteen minutes later we arrived at the spring to find the place, as usual, crowded with people. There were also cattle, which was very unusual.

We set up our meager camp about a mile from the spring near a tall, rocky cliff. I was surprised to see many wild pigeons roosting on the cliff. We soon collected a few of them for lunch with the .22 rifle that Ed and I brought with us.

It was late in the afternoon when a young native came into our camp. Through our guide we began to ask him about oudad, or barbary sheep as they are usually called. The young fellow indicated there were many in the mountains behind our camp. He said he could show us some in a very short time. I jumped at the opportunity, and Guy agreed to go along. So off we went, skirting the base of the hill, then cutting up when we found a ravine that was not too steep. After an hour we were out of the trees and brush and into rockier terrain covered by small patches of grass.

We had just rounded several large rocks when our guide stopped and pointed ahead. I could see the backs of two animals but could not see their heads because they were grazing on the grass between the rocks. As we

An addax gallops across the Sahara Desert near Fada.

waited, a herd of barbary sheep grazed out from behind the rocks not more than 100 yards from us. I checked them over with my binoculars and found only one suitable ram. He was not as good as I wanted, but we were each allowed two animals, so I shot him.

He measured out at 25 inches, which is a respectable head, but I was not satisfied. For the next five days we climbed the low hills looking for a better one. Ed Chatwell was more successful. On the first day out, he climbed a low hill with Claude and looked down upon a lone ram. He made a fine

The barbary sheep that roam the hills of the Chad make a handsome trophy.

trophy, indeed. Its 29-inch horns were very heavy at the base and broomed off at the tip.

We came upon an unusual sight in these hills. On several flat plateaus there were many mounds of rocks. Claude asked the local man if these were burial places of their dead, and the man said no. He explained the markers were the burial places of the "Old Ones", long before his people arrived. They were a different race of people. He would not go near the mounds. We could only suppose that in the distant past, some ancient tribe of Arabic or Egyptian people had lived here, buried their people on the flat rock plateau and covered them with stones. The markers will, no doubt, remain for centuries to come — a fitting tribute to a hardy group of people who lived in this harsh land.

We saw many barbary sheep but none satisfied our expectations. Claude and I even slept out in the sand of dry nulla one night in order to get an early start in the morning. But until the fifth day, when our supplies were exhausted and we were reduced to eating wild meat and very little of anything else, were we able to find a ram.

I shot him at a long distance, probably over 400 yards, and broke his front leg. We trailed him over the rocks for five hours until locating him below a rock ledge with some other sheep. When he ran out, I shot him again, ending my hunt for a good barbary sheep. He, too, measured 29 inches, but did not have the good bases of Ed's ram. However, he was a fine specimen.

We loaded up and headed back to Oom Chalouba with Claude and I in the front Rover, Ed and Guy in the second Rover. Ed had put away his rifle saying the hunt was over. But I make a practice of never putting my rifle away until I am within sight of a town.

I was pleased with all my trophies. Thirteen made the record book, but I was not too happy with my two scimitar oryx which measured almost 42 and 43 inches. We had given up seeing any oryx because we were 300 miles to the south of their area.

I was half-dozing in the heat of the day on the rough road when Claude remarked, "Some animals are coming on our right; see the dust?"

I awoke and watched the small cloud come closer. Suddenly seven scimitar oryx emerged from the dust and crossed the old road about 500 yards ahead of us. The last one had horns that curved back until the tips were lower than his back.

"My God, look at the oryx," I shouted.

Claude slammed the Land Rover to a stop and before I could get out, he was already disconnecting the trailer from the rear of our vehicle.

"Jump in. Let's go get him . . . . that's the best one by far."

We both jumped back into the Rover and let the tongue of the trailer drop into the sand. We roared away after the dust cloud that was rapidly disappearing into the distance.

We gained steadily on the oryx. Soon I could see the flashing black horns bobbing above the graceful bodies as they plunged forward. There were seven bulls, all good, but the one at the rear of the herd was outstanding.

We came up behind them going full speed, ignoring the fact that we may

Unfortunately, sights such as this one are vanishing fast in the land of the Chad.

hit a hole or ditch. When we were within 70 or 80 yards of the last animal, Claude shouted, "Ready?"

"Ready," I yelled, bracing myself for the quick stop. I almost hit the dashboard when Claude jammed on the brakes. I righted myself, jerked open the door and practically fell into the desert sand.

The oryx, going at full speed, were about 125 to 150 yards away before I could get on the big male, but at the crack of the .300 Weatherby, the animal just collapsed. The rear end shot, if placed right, is one of the most lethal shots that a hunter can make.

My tape came out of my pocket quickly while Claude held up the beautiful head. I put the tape on the horns. He measured 46 inches and would be one of the top scimitar oryx in the book. Of course, he would shrink a little.

"Well done," Claude smiled. "I am glad we could get a good one for you."

Ed and Guy drove up and came over to inspect the horns.

"How big?" Ed inquired.

"Forty-six inches," Claude answered.

"You lucky devil," Ed said, smiling and shaking my hand like the good sport he is.

"Not lucky, Ed, just ready," I replied. "Remember when I tell you I'm not finished and be ready for anything that happens."

We skinned out the oryx, loaded the meat into the Rover and headed back to Oom Chalouba. Guy and Ed had brought along our trailer. The desert took on the usual rosy glow that comes with sunset, a little later turning the hot desert into a beautiful fairyland of color. We camped that night, and the stars hung so low I almost felt that I could reach out and grab one.

Claude pointed out a sputnik that was following its orbit around the earth. A bright spot passing among other bright spots that were distant planets — the new and old in a world that is changing much too fast, too soon.

7

Learning from mistakes in Mozambique

Mozambique is a Portuguese colony that had produced some fantastic trophies in years prior to my arrival, and I looked forward to hunting there. Yet it is also one of the areas where the meat hunter has been the busiest. Thousands of tons of wild meat have been transported into South Africa in the form of "Biltong" and sold to ranchers for the natives working in the fields.

However, much of this wild meat has found its way into the cities of Durbin, Johannesburg, and Capetown. The South African was the originator of Biltong and loves it.

I have talked to many old professional hunters, both Portuguese and South African, who admitted killing thousands of species for meat, ranging from elephant to antelope.

Most of these men admitted they preferred to shoot elephant and buffalo rather than the antelope because of the large quantity of meat that the two species would yield. Another hunter told me he had shot complete herds of waterbuck, a stupid animal that does not spook easily. The herds included females and their young. Yet the greatest havoc was wrought among the herds of elephant and buffalo.

Opening pages and opposite: The herds of elephant in Mozambique are scarce, yet we hoped to get a chance at some of them.

Perhaps this is why, except for a few isolated cases, the ivory is very poor and very few big heads of buffalo are taken in Mozambique.

My first safari to Mozambique was for twenty-one days. My outfitter was Jose Ruiz, who told me that I would be free to move around from one camp to another and be assured of a good hunt.

My arrival in Lourenco Marques was uneventful. I was met by Jose and his brother-in-law and partner, Vasco Cartega, a very engaging person with an outgoing personality. Jose and Vasco were the complete opposite in appearance and personality. Jose was very thin and dark while Vasco was somewhat on the portly side with a light complexion. Both smiled easily, but while Jose was quiet and reserved, Vasco was exuberant and talked continuously.

The trip from Lourenco Marques to the hunting area is about a seven-hour ride on the small railway that runs from Mozambique to Rhodesia. It is, by far, the easiest way to get there.

I was met by my professional hunter, a handsome young Portuguese chap with a difficult name I found almost impossible to pronounce. After trying several times without correctly saying it, he interrupted. "Just call me Joe. I like that name." So "Joe" it was, for the next twenty-one days.

We arrived at Lilaua camp in about two hours after leaving the railroad station. It was a lovely camp, possibly the best I have ever seen. It was a cluster of small, round mud-plastered cottages covered with whitewash that gave them a clean, pleasant look. They sat on concrete slabs about eight inches off the ground. Electricity was furnished by a small power plant. The inside of the cottages was clean and neat. Hot and cold water was available in the modern bathroom.

Outside, the grounds around the camp were swept clean of all leaves and other debris usually found under the trees. Fifty yards away, the jungle stood ready to devour this small spot that had been cleared on the bank of the Limpopo River in the heart of Mozambique.

We arrived at about 11 A.M. and after an excellent lunch, drove down river in the open Toyota that Joe used for a hunting car, to look over some of the hunting area.

"The Kruger Park lies over that way about fifteen miles," Joe said. "We will go over near the boundary and look for a good elephant in a few days."

"I would prefer a good kudu and nyalla," I answered.

"We'll get them too, but you will probably never get closer to the Kruger than this."

"O.K.," I said. "You are the boss."

On our way back, we took a young male impala for camp meat. Although I saw two nyalla, neither was worth taking, and the small herd of sable offered no better than about a 35-inch head.

I asked Joe about leopard and lion, but he indicated that his area was not too good for either animal. He thought the camp across the Chobe from us, "Squalla-Squalla," might produce a leopard because several had been taken there. I remarked to Joe that leopard were bound to roam along the river, but I wasn't sure of lion.

The next ten days were usual for the African safari. Most of the time was spent driving the Toyota along the narrow roads made by the Williamson Diamond Company. The thick bush had been cleared where the company had used a heavy bulldozer to carve out paths to possible diamond deposits. Similar roads had been created during oil exploration in Alaska and other parts of North America.

Mozambique is covered with very thick bush and rarely could we drive across country as we could in Kenya, Tanganyika and most other African countries. How hunters traveled before the diamond hunters made the roads was a puzzle to me. Unless they walked a lot, not too much ground could be covered.

There was plenty of game, but we never saw much of it at one time because the bush was too thick. When an animal was sighted, we left the Toyota and proceeded on foot. I was lucky to see half the herd before the wind would shift or one of the animals would spot us. I did manage to collect nyalla, Southern impala, greater kudu and lesser game, but nothing was really outstanding.

We followed several herds of elephant, but found nothing worth shooting. Joe was getting a little disgusted and, for that matter, so was I, when we came upon a large bull track.

It didn't take us long to decide to follow the bull. Taking a large canteen of water, we plunged into the bush in pursuit of the animal with the big feet. It was hot and getting hotter by the hour.

Some six hours and 14 miles later, the bull joined up with a small herd. We proceeded ahead even more cautiously. The spoor was very fresh and the droppings were still warm.

Another hour and we had caught up with the herd. We maneuvered

Mozambique did yield a greater kudu with a good pair of horns.

around the animals dozing on their feet during the hottest part of the day.

It took quite a while to locate the bull in the thick bush, but finally we were within 20 feet and directly in front of him. He was behind a thick clump of bush and I could barely make out his head.

I looked at Joe, who nodded, as his hands indicated the tusks were quite thick. He had been studying the brute through his binoculars. I looked again at the bull, trying to get a glimpse of the tusks. I could see one protruded past his lip about two feet and ended in a ragged stump. The tusk was quite big in circumference, but very short in length.

I indicated this to Joe by measuring a short distance between my hand and the gun. He nodded, but indicated that the other tusk was quite long. In Mozambique the ivory does not come big, so I felt I'd better shoot this one. Besides, I never argue with a professional on his home ground. I have always felt that if you do, you are paying him for nothing because he is supposed to be an expert in what he is doing. I raised the .458, centering it on his forehead, and squeezed off.

The results were typical. The elephant squealed and rushed about. I was totally unexpected for the bull's next move, however. He whirled away from me and crashed through the jungle. I only had a second to give him a parting body shot.

When the noise had abated and the elephant had gone, Joe looked at me and shook his head sadly. "You missed the brain," he stated, which was quite obvious.

We started on the trail of the bull again. Within another hour we caught up with him. He had left the herd and was standing in a thicket. Facing downward, he forced us to approach him head on. Again I blasted him in the skull through the bush, and again he bolted away. Joe just shook his head sadly, and took up the trail, the tall skinny tracker leading the way.

We walked about a quarter of a mile and were going round some thick leafy clumps of bush when the lead tracker suddenly turned and bolted past us, almost knocking me over in the process. Joe and I stepped to one side so we could see around the thick clump of bush. Instantly, we both threw up our rifles and fired into the head of the bull elephant facing us.

The shots were pure reflex, fired under pressure by both of us. The bull was stone dead. He had died on his front knees with his hind legs bent behind him, yet he still towered above us. Before dying, he had turned around in his tracks and was evidently waiting for us.

I could hardly believe my eyes when I looked at him. The tusk I had seen through the bush was about two feet long. The other tusk was even shorter and broken just at the gum line. Suddenly I was a bit angry with Joe.

"Why in the hell did you let me shoot this animal?" I demanded. Joe examined the tusk, then the feet of the animal before answering.

"Wrong bull," he announced with conviction.

"Not so!" I said. "I remember that tusk."

"No," he insisted. "We followed the wrong bull and you must have shot another one the second time."

"The hell I did," I answered. "How many shots should this animal have in the head? Four, right?"

I stepped close to the bull's head and, after careful inspection, pointed out four holes in the rough hide of his forehead. Two were close together in a line near the center of the forehead and two more were a little higher in the skull. One bullet had penetrated the back of the skull. I had been close to the bull and should have shot very low, just where his trunk connected with his head. The lucky bullet in the rib section was the killing shot, but it took him a little time to die.

Joe had nothing more to say as we started back to the Toyota. The two hours it took to return had exhausted our water supply and that Toyota sure looked good to me. It had been a very hard and disappointing day.

Early next morning I shot a good chobe bushbuck near the river. Joe decided we would hang the carcass up for leopard bait. The process took almost an hour and I was an interested spectator. I am very fond of leopard. I think this animal is the most fascinating and dangerous of the big cats. I have hunted them with some of the best professional hunters in East Africa where leopard baiting has become an art. However, I didn't offer one word of advice. In my opinion, I would have been out of line.

Three days earlier we had hung a shoulder of a buffalo up for a leopard bait, and I had been very critical of the procedure used. Joe had selected a short stubby tree with limbs not more than eight feet from the ground. I thought to myself that a lion will surely get that bait if there is one in the country. Sure enough, on the second night a lioness climbed the tree, ripped the bait loose and dropped it to the ground for her half-grown cub. Now as I watched Joe set up this second bait, I could tell he didn't know the first thing about baiting for leopard. I intended to enlighten him for his own good, but not until I was ready to leave. He was a nice guy and I liked him. He just didn't know a damn thing about leopards.

The days flew by as they usually do when I am on a hunting trip.

The days were quite routine except for one morning when a boy killed a puff adder coiled just below the front step of my rondaavel, when he came to wake me up. They are a deadly snake and I might have had an unpleasant surprise when I stepped off the edge of the concrete slab on my way to breakfast, had he not been killed.

I didn't see a single lion while I was in Mozambique, and although there were signs of leopard, none came to the bushbuck that hung by the river.

We crossed over to the other side and hunted the area around the Esqualla-Esqualla camp where I took a fair impala. But all in all, the Mozambique hunt was not nearly as good as I thought it would be.

Then came the last day of the safari. While driving along the river early in the morning, one of the boys turned to speak to Joe. He stopped the Toyota and we got out to take a look.

A body of an animal had been dragged across the path. We started following the drag, and within a few steps, the pug marks of a big leopard were clearly etched in the loose dirt.

A few yards away the body had caught on a big limb and the short brown hair of an impala clung to a small spot of freshly dried blood. A leopard had killed an impala and had dragged him away to eat him.

I pushed a shell into the chamber of my .300 Weatherby, as we continued to follow the drag as quietly as possible.

We were approaching a very big baobab tree, 30 feet in circumference, that towered over the other shorter trees. Before we arrived at the spot, I already felt the dead impala would be in the tree. I hoped the cat would still be there.

I am sure he was, but had either seen us coming or heard us and made a quick retreat. Wedged firmly in the fork of a huge limb, was the young male impala he had left behind.

After a short conference, it was decided to leave two of the boys at the tree to build a blind and we would go hunting. We were not far from the camp and the boys could return when finished. Joe and I, together with another man and the driver, drove off to see what we could find. At 8 P.M. we were scheduled to cross the river and catch a train to Lourenco Marques.

We hunted all day and even stopped in camp for lunch, where Joe questioned the boys about building the blind. They assured him that everything was ready, so we returned to the hunt.

We didn't shoot anything. Just before sunset we headed back for the big baobab, parking the Toyota about half a mile away. To say I was disappointed when I saw the blind was an understatement. I was furious. It was the poorest job I had ever seen.

The boys had cut a few pieces of brush and stood them in a circle almost directly under the tree. The cover was so skimpy that any cat could see a man in it, 10 yards away. But worst of all, without a roof on the blind, the leopard could look right down on top of us when he climbed the tree.

"The dumb bastards," I swore.

"The blind looks all right to me," Joe said. "I have brought a light, he won't come 'til dark."

"That's where you are wrong," I said. "This is not a bait, this is the leopard's kill and he will come anytime to claim it. I am surprised that he isn't here now."

I took out the folding knife I always carry and began cutting branches for the top of the circle. Joe reluctantly started helping me. Within 10 minutes we had enough of a roof so that if we leaned forward, the leopard couldn't see us. We sat down to wait for his coming.

The sun dipped below the horizon and the forest was in silence except for a small flock of birds flying down to the river. All was still until suddenly a baboon barked to the right of us and was joined by several others. I touched knees with Joe. The leopard was moving. All was still again. Then I heard

The impala and nyala were just a beginning in Mozambique. We were on our way for leopard.

the twittering of birds in the thick bush to our right. The leopard had come.

The big baobab grew in an open space that was clear of bush on three sides. However, on one side, low bush grew almost up to the tree. Here the boys had built the blind. The birds continued to twitter for a few moments while Joe and I remained frozen. Behind us and quite near, the leopard growled. Neither of us moved; I barely breathed. I knew that the cat knew we were there, but could do nothing about it. He would either climb the tree or go away.

The sun completed its descent and twilight was upon us before I heard him again. This time he was in front of us and didn't care if we knew it.

He growled, walking back and forth under the tree in the darkness. I leaned forward in the blind and mentally said, "Go up the tree, you bastard. Go up the tree." Then in the stillness of the early darkness, I heard the ripple of his claws hitting the bark of the tree as his powerful legs lifted him into the tree and up to the first fork, 20 feet off the ground.

He stopped, and without seeing him, I knew he was sitting in the fork of the tree, staring down upon his domain with fierce eyes.

Then I heard the soft whisper of his movement again as he went further into the tree. I raised my head and looked up just in time to see him walk out in fluid motion on the big limb and pause directly over his kill.

I had a Bushnell Scopechief on my rifle with a thick post that can be used when shooting in dim light. When it began to get dark, I had silently screwed the cap off and raised the post. Now I lifted my rifle and settled the scope on the sky just above the cat. The post stood out sharp and clear. I brought the gun down until I could see the top of the post just under his chest, then raised it a fraction and brought it over to the right another fraction, and squeezed her off.

At the explosion, the big cat dropped out of the limb like a sack of salt. Joe exclaimed, "Hey! Why did you do that?"

"Why not," I answered. "Didn't you see me aiming?"

"Yes, but I thought you were just trying to see him. I have a light here."

"Joe, don't you realize if the cat had laid down on that big limb, the only part of him we would see would be the top of his hips and shoulders. I shot him because it was the only chance I would get."

"Did you kill him?" he asked.

"I think so. It was a good shot and he dropped down; he didn't jump. Let's go see."

Cautiously we moved under the tree while Joe played the light ahead of us. There, in a golden spotted heap, he lay just as he had dropped off the limb, stone dead.

A quick examination revealed a neat bullet hole in his right shoulder where the leg joined the body. The hole in the top of the left shoulder showed where the 180 grain nosler had emerged. I couldn't have hit him better if I had placed the bullet there by hand.

Joe reached for my hand. "That was very well done!" he said simply. The boys came up with the Toyota. We loaded the cat into the back and went back to camp with only an hour to make the train.

While driving to the depot, I asked Joe if he could stand a little advice from an older man. He stated that he could.

"Do you know why you didn't get a hit on that Bushbuck bait we put up?"

"No, why?"

"Well, let me tell you what was wrong with the whole setup," I said. "In the first place, you picked a tree completely out in the open without any cover. A leopard seldom walks out in the open when he is hunting unless it is a big plain. He will always use cover. Even if a leopard had hit the bait, he would only return after dark because he had no cover. Never bait a tree that does not have at least cover up to within six to eight feet on one side. The exception, of course, is a lone tree that is out on the plains whenever leopard go to hunt. Also," I continued, "you hung the bait on the east side of the tree which is bad because the sun sets in the west. You can see the bait at least 15 minutes longer and many times that makes the difference."

"Another point, you did not clear out the limbs and leaves behind the bait. As you have seen tonight, if a man is using a post in his scope, he can still shoot accurately even after it is too dark to see below, if he knows what he's doing."

"I remember one more thing you could have done better and that was the drag. Your man dragged the guts only a short distance along the river bank. I would have had two drags — the guts and the stomach with a small hole in it — and dragged all the way to the water and out from the tree with the second drag for at least a half mile. Leopard often follow a river because it is where the thick bush will grow. I hope I have been some help."

He sat for a moment without speaking, then said, "What you say makes sense; I'll remember it."

As I have said, I never criticize a pro, but oftentimes I see them do things that are very wrong. I will pass along information I have learned either by seeing it done by top people or learning myself the hard way. Either learning process is an expensive one.

8

The McElroy Trophy Room

C.J. McElroy's collection of trophies is a legend among the hunting fraternity the world over—more for big-game hunting than any man on earth. His Trophy Room—a veritable museum of big-game wildlife—contain 236 specimens of the taxidermist's skill.

So informative and educational is his Trophy Room that many organizations, such as the Boy and Girl Scouts, Y.M.C.A., grammar and high-school classes—even adult education groups—have viewed this rare and extensive collection of Nature's creations.

The McElroy Trophy Room

It is located in his home north of Tucson, Arizona and has been viewed by thousands of individuals. The collection of trophies are from five continents, including ninety-seven different species of African game alone. All twenty-six species of legal big game of North America appear in the collection which also features three Grand Slams of sheep.

There are also animals from Australia, New Zealand, India, Iran, Mongolia, South America, Mexico, Alaska and five provinces of Canada.

The collection is the result of twenty-six trips to Africa, hunting twenty-five countries, three trips to India, seven trips to Alaska, four trips to Mexico and extensive hunting in the United States.

The ibex of Sudan

The Red Sea is probably most famous as the body of water that opened at Moses' command to let the Jewish people pass in safety out of Egypt, then closed to cover the Egyptian army chasing them.

Today the Red Sea is becoming well known for another reason among hunters. The great Nubian ibex can be found surrounding low, hot, rocky hills from Port Sudan to the Erietran border in Ethiopia.

The area is also famous in English history because of the fuzzy wuzzy tribesmen who inhabited these same hills. With only thin daggers, curved swords and sheer guts, the tribes managed to put up a good fight against the British and their modern firearms. They were great defenders of their land, and the English had to resort to a large degree of fire power and many trained soldiers to defeat them.

Dr. Ed Chatwell and I arrived in Port Sudan by way of Khartoum in August. We had probably selected the hottest time of the year to hunt Nubian ibex. We were met by George Zafario, a young Greek who directed safaris for Sudan Safaris, whose owner Ozis Osman lived in Khartoum.

A personable young man, George was born in the Sudan below

Opening pages: The graceful giraffe of the plains were a great contrast to the rocky hills of the Sudan, seen on the opposite page. Here silent markers pinpoint where warriors died fighting for the land surrounding the Red Sea.

Khartoum. He had moved to Port Sudan several years earlier and knew the people and the country well. It took a day to clear through the local police, then we were on our way along the thin strip of blacktop the English had built during their occupation. It weaved along the edge of the Red Sea from Port Sudan to Tokar and into Ethiopia. We left the paved road after about 10 miles when we decided it would be easier to travel through the desert. The hard top had deteriorated to the point where flash floods from the mountains had carved holes 10 feet wide in the hard surface. Some of these holes were 3 and 4 feet deep. The Sudanese had done no maintainence work on the road since their independence from the British almost a decade ago. Pounded by the big trucks carrying supplies and merchandise between eastern Sudan and Ethiopia, the road gradually grew worse until the desert was considered a much safer place to drive. As the ruts in the desert road grew deeper, the trucks moved further out into the desert. Sometimes we were a mile from the broken paved strip.

It was a lovely drive despite the bad road. We passed several caravans of camels and a few herds of goats going to market in Port Sudan, the main seaport and largest town in Eastern Sudan. We also passed the ancient city of Suakin which had served as the main seaport of the Red Sea many centuries ago. For hundreds of years, Arab dhows and vessels came into this port bearing everything from human slaves to precious gems. It was an open port and a very busy one.

It was the home of many wealthy sheiks and government officers. Some of the houses were three stories high. A magnificent old fort with antique cannons and many statues was proof that the city had once been the seat of power in the Sudan. Now there is only rot and decay. The cannons are stilled, the people are gone. Only the walls of the roofless houses still stand. A few stray camels and goats nibble at bits of greenery. This is all that remains of once beautiful, well cared for hedges and flower gardens of the ancient sheiks.

A few fishermen had built shacks of rusty tin and palm shrouds along the Red Sea. We stopped and bought some fresh fish for a few shillings. George explained that we would be in camp within three hours, where we would have a fish dinner.

In the distance, three palm trees came into view. As we approached the spot, we found it to be a small village oasis. People were busy drawing water by hand from three wells. It would then be emptied into narrow wooden troughs. Goats and camels fought for their share, occasionally dodging a blow from a Sudanese when they stayed too long.

We stopped in the village where George could drink some of the black coffee which Ed and I refused. Ed got out his polaroid camera while I set up my 16 mm camera to take some pictures. Suddenly our first fuzzy wuzzy appeared. He was a young boy in his late teens, accompanied by an older man. Both were tall and lean with thin aristocratic features, bold black eyes and hair that surrounded their heads like a large, black ball of fine, kinky steel. Both carried curved swords in a leather scabbard and each had a dagger stuck in his belt.

They strolled silently into the black crowd that had gathered around Ed, who was busy taking pictures with his polaroid. The crowd parted reluctantly as the two men came closer for a look at the photography equipment. Ed snapped a picture of the young man, then showed it to him after it had developed. Without a word, the young man took it, but when Ed reached for it, he wouldn't give it back. Then the others began clamoring for pictures. Things got a little rough as Ed was shoved around by the angry crowd. George left his chair under the shade of the coffee shop and pushed his way toward us. "Quick, let's all get back into the Land Rovers." I was only too glad to comply. I had over $2,000 invested in my camera equipment.

The crowd was still shouting demands and attempting to detain us as we drove away. It was an indication of how primitive the people still were. I had never had such an incident occur before in East Africa.

We arrived in camp about 4 P.M. It consisted of two sleeping tents and a mess tent. Ed and I were to share a tent. They had been set up in a dry wash at the foot of a range of low barren hills. In the distance, a larger range began and disappeared in the distance. Some peaks were several thousand feet high. They were completely bare of trees and shrubs. In the washes along the foothills where we had camped, clumps of heavy-leaved bushes dotted the area.

A group of natives were camped nearby. Shortly after we arrived, some of them drifted into our camp. They were fuzzie wuzzies and resembled the two men we saw in the village. A few of them had an added attraction — small rolls of dirt covered with camel or sheep grease, dangling on thin strands of fine wire from their hair. The smell of rancid grease and unwashed bodies is quite a combination, especially in the hot climate we

At right: The fuzzy wuzzy tribesmen were thin, with bold eyes and large crops of hair. Below: George Zafaroi of Sudan Safaris goes shopping for fish which had just been caught from the Red Sea.

were all forced to endure. I dropped off to sleep that night dreaming of ibex jumping from rock to rock, rather than sheep jumping over fences.

Next morning we were ready to go long before daylight. We took only one vehicle, which soon developed into a problem. The guide of the fuzzy wuzzies insisted that he ride in the front seat to direct George through the dry wash where we would be hunting. This wouldn't have been a problem except only three could ride up front and the back was enclosed. When I looked inside, there were about 10 fuzzy wuzzies; I was going to have to ride with them if Ed was to ride up front. I climbed in back, taking short breaths for a few minutes until I became accustomed to the smell.

We drove about 30 minutes over fairly rough ground. I was more than happy when we stopped and I could climb out of the back and into the brisk chill of the early morning desert. Around me, the rocky peaks stood against the dark sky. The fuzzy wuzzies piled out quietly and quickly disappeared into the darkness. George, Ed and I along with the head man, started through the canyon. We walked for about an hour at an easy pace, then started climbing the side of a canyon wall using two flashlights we had brought with us. In another 20 minutes we were up some 200 feet above the sandy bottom of the canyon, and settled behind some good-sized rocks. Dawn was just breaking, and the morning light behind us promised another clear, hot day.

Across the narrow canyon, 300 yards from us, a tall peak rose twice the height of our side. It was also much higher than any point around us, ending in a sharp jumble of sheer rock at the top. In the early morning light, the gradual outline of the mountain could be seen clearly against the blue sky behind us.

Suddenly a small figure appeared at the very top of the mountain and gave a wailing cry. Immediately, other figures appeared along the slopes of both canyon walls, answering the original cries. Then the top figure began to descend, followed by other nearby figures until a thin line of men moved together down the mountain. It was quite an interesting experience watching the fuzzy wuzzies effectively drive the ibex off the peak. If some animals tried to turn around the side of the mountain again, a figure appeared to drive them back. A few big ibex were not to be denied, however, their long, black, curved horns glistening in the early morning rays of sunlight as they disappeared over a ridge.

The others jumped from rock to rock and down the sheer cliffs

The ancient city of Suakin was once the main seaport of the Red Sea, but today most of the large houses of wealthy sheiks are in ruin where camels nibble the remains of tended gardens.

encouraged by rock-throwing natives and their small, yellow dogs.

There must have been at least 200 male, female and young ibex on the mountain as Ed and I watched them come down through our binoculars. Most were females and young, but there were a few young billies. Occasionally, a good one would race across the face of the mountain. It was difficult to keep close watch on him to determine the size of his horns, as he darted in and out among the rocks.

The men had advanced about half-way down, when a big old billy came out of a shallow cave and ran at an angle toward the bottom of the canyon. He looked very good to me, so I tried a shot at about 300 yards. I didn't lead him enough and saw dust fly about two feet behind him. I led him a little more and shot below him. He stopped for a moment, then rolled down the mountain where he came to rest against a rock.

The flood of ibex came off the mountain, down into the bottom of the canyon, spread out and disappeared over the ridges. Now and then, one would run down and disappear until there was none left in sight. The beaters or drivers were still yelling on the side of the mountain.

"What are they yelling about?" I asked George.

He, in turn, asked the head man who answered, "There is a big billy in a cave and won't come out."

The animal interested me and I asked George if they could see him. Again he questioned the chief, who stood up and yelled across the canyon.

"Yes," he said to George. "He is a big billy; they can see him."

A deserted cannon which once protected the city is now covered with rust.

I made up my mind in a hurry. "I'm going to climb up and take a look at him," I said.

The four of us came down to the floor of the canyon. While Ed and the chief remained, George and I started climbing up the other side where we were soon joined by a young tribesman who moved up the cliff as agile as a monkey.

The slope face was known as "Rotten Rock." Sometimes a piece of it would come loose when I grabbed an edge to pull myself up. After a short time, George turned back, saying it was too dangerous to continue. But the fuzzy wuzzy and I kept moving up the slope. He took my rifle and slung it across his back as we continued to climb.

Within a half hour we were about 125 yards below the small group of men who had gathered near the cave. We stopped on a small spot below a smooth stretch of rock about 10 feet wide that offered nothing to hold on to. I could see that we could not go further unless we found a rougher spot to negotiate.

Above me, the men were pointing below the ledge on which they were standing, but I could not see because of the smooth rock in front of me. I lifted one foot and motioned for the young man to raise me up. He understood instantly, making a circle with his hands. He hoisted me up about three feet so I could clear the smooth ledge in front of us. By the time my head cleared the top of the rock, my binoculars were in my hand and to my eyes. A quick look was all I needed to take in the situation.

Above me, the mountain face was concave and pitted with small shallow caves. The men couldn't possibly get down around the ledge on which they stood. The only way they could see into the shallow caves was by going to one side about 300 yards from where they were now standing. All they could do was roll rocks over the top of the cave and hope it would cause the remaining ibex to come out into the open. He was a stubborn one that refused to be stampeded.

I located him in another moment. He was big billy, all right. He stood against the wall of the cave. I watched as a native rolled a rock on the roof of his cave and bounced into space. The ibex shook his head and stamped his front feet but refused to move. I spoke to the man holding me against the rock and, again, he understood perfectly. It's strange indeed that hunters do not need to speak to each other in the same language. He lowered me down instantly. I took off my binoculars and picked up my rifle, jacked a shell into the chamber and indicated to the young man that I wanted to be raised up again.

He lifted me up until I could lie with my chest on the top of the ledge. I centered the cross hairs on the front edge of the ibex's shoulder, steadied it a moment while the small knot of silent men above watched, and squeezed off.

The recoil of the .300 Weatherby moved me back on the smooth rock a few inches, but the youngster below held firm. I watched the big billy leap into space, somersault once, land on a rock pile, then bounce into space and disappear below. Wild cries could be heard from the men above me, who were jumping up and down with excitement.

The young man lowered me to the ground and stepped away from me, smiling. There was a certain air of new respect in his manner as I held out my hand and thanked him for his help. It was a much longer way down because neither of us trusted the slippery rock. We cut across the face of the mountain until we reached the ridge at a lower level and followed it down. The excitement was gone and the adrenalin had slowed down to a normal pace. In about an hour, we were back with George and Ed who had been joined by the other men. They had brought down the billy that I had shot, but unfortunately, the big, black horns had shattered completely on the rocks. I felt bad about this, but George quickly pointed out the men were very happy to have the meat. Besides, he added, there were plenty of ibex and I could shoot another.

By 11 A.M. the sun had started heating the rock around us, turning the canyon into an oven. The temperature would reach well over 100 degrees in another hour and remain high until late afternoon. We returned to the Toyota, where the chief again insisted on sitting up front while I rode in the back with the fuzzy wuzzies. The smell hadn't improved.

During the next three days, our drives were not too productive, bringing only a few ibex, but no good billies. Poor Ed's feet were covered with blisters. He had a hard time of it, but the old boy has courage to keep on going. On the fourth day we arose earlier than usual and drove a long distance before coming to a large canyon. We entered on foot, plowing through sand three and four inches deep.

We came to a location where two smaller canyons merged to become a large gorge. Located in the center of these two canyons was a rocky island that rose about 200 feet. We stopped as George indicated that the drivers would come up from both directions from the smaller canyons.

"Ed, why don't you get up on the top of that knoll?" I asked. "You can see into both canyons."

Look closely at this rugged mountain face and see if you can spot a few ibex.

145

"Do you think it's a good spot?" he asked.

"I sure do," I answered. "I'll go on a ways so I won't disturb you." He was climbing the knoll when I left, hobbling on his sore feet.

I selected a spot about 500 yards away, facing a tall peak where I felt some ibex lived, then settled down to await the beaters.

The sun was just rising when they came running and shouting down the two small canyons and over the peak. First, I saw some females, young kids and two young billies, then came a pretty good male, but I turned him down. Suddenly I heard four shots from the spot Ed had taken his stand, then silence.

The men came down and joined me. The chief was disappointed that I had not shot some meat for him and stalked off in Ed's direction. I followed him. In a few minutes we came upon Ed, who was standing by a dead ibex, smiling from ear to ear with his ever-ready polaroid.

"I shot two, Mac," he said.

"So I see," I answered. I turned the billy over to check the size of his horns. "Damn," I exclaimed. "This is a hell of an ibex."

"Do you think so?" Ed asked.

"I know so. I don't know how good, but he is very good."

I took my tape out and laid it on the heavy ridged horns. They exceeded 46 inches. "Ed, I think you just shot a world record," I said.

And so it almost was, measuring second in Rowland Ward Record Book of big game. The record, killed almost fifty years earlier, was retained by the Loder collection.

Ed's second ibex also proved to be very good, measuring well over 40 inches. Ed was thrilled, and I was very pleased that he had taken two good trophies.

The next day he asked me if I would care if he returned to Port Sudan. I assured him I didn't, and that he would be more comfortable there than in the field.

The next five days I took a good dik-dik and a good ibex that measured 43-5/8 inches. I also managed to take a short but uneventful trip into northern Eritrea, stopping at the border check point and telling them we wanted to shoot an Eritrean gazelle.

I shot one on the first day and returned through the small town of Tokar to our camp at the foot of the sunbaked hills surrounding the Red Sea. The next day I joined Ed in Port Sudan for the trip back to Khartoum and home.

The days of mountain climbing pay off and result in these record breaking ibex.

Ethiopia and its exotic animals

The beautiful antelope with lyre-shaped horns sailed off the cliff and over the tops of the green trees, twenty feet below, in a last convulsive jump. He was dead in mid-air as he crashed into the treetops and disappeared from sight. When the sound of his falling stopped, there was silence in the jungle for a moment. Then the forest reverberated again, but this time with cries of success and triumph from four black men and a Swiss yelling in unison. We had taken a mountain nyala — one of the rarest and most beautiful antelopes in the world.

Ethiopia! Even the name sounds mysterious and ominous. And so it has been to the white man for centuries.

Many times he has invaded this land and, on occasion, subdued some of the tribes. But he has never conquered the entire country. Thus this black country is one of the oldest civilizations and kingdoms in the world. The word "civilization" should be used loosely when speaking of this interesting part of the world because, even today, there are places where the white man is not welcome. Even black men from other regions are sometimes looked upon with suspicion and open hostility.

Sportsmen were hunting this territory (at one time known as Abyssinia)

Opening pages: A quiet herd of gazelle graze in an open glade in Ethiopia. Opposite page: A rare white eared kob, one of Ethiopia's exotic animals.

long before Kenya and other East African countries became the favorite hunting place for big game by the blue bloods and royalty of Europe.

The black-maned lions and black leopards of Abyssinia were the favorite pets in the Egyptian Pharoah's palaces on the Nile. In the arenas of Rome, the Ethiopians' lions killed the Christians to please Caesar and bloodthirsty crowds. The black-maned lion and black leopard still exist in Ethiopia today, but not in the large numbers found centuries ago. The people have mellowed to an extent. White men are allowed to hunt their country without being strung up to a post and castrated, a favorite treatment given strangers in the interior not too long ago.

My safari to Ethiopia was not to hunt the black-maned lion or the black leopard, but to hunt four of the most exotic animals in Africa — the mountain nyala, menelik bushbuck, Nile lechwe and white-eared kob. These animals are indeed rare, not only because they are few in number, but because they are confined to certain areas. The white-eared kob and Nile lechwe are found in the swamps along the borders of Ethiopia and the Sudan. The menelik bushbuck and mountain nyala are only seen high in the interior mountains of Ethiopia. There are fewer mountain nyala hanging in trophy rooms of the world today than any other major African animal, including the bongo.

I hunted Ethiopia in January with Karl Luthy. We had one of the most successful safaris ever recorded in that country. In forty-five days, we took the four most important animals — the mountain nyala, bushbuck, white-eared kob and Nile lechwe. We also took eight other species of game from other areas, a total of twelve animals making the record book.

We left Addis Ababa early in the morning in Karl's jeep, bound for a small village called Bedessa. It is located 300 miles near the eastern tip of Somali in the Arushi Mountains. We passed through ancient villages with the strange-sounding names of Debre, Zeit, Nazareth and Asbe Tafari. These settlements are several hundred years old and unchanged by the passing of time.

We spent some time in Awash Park, the halfway point, before arriving in Bedessa late in the afternoon. Heavy clouds that had gathered over the mountains opened and rain began to fall just as we entered the village.

We were followed by Karl's heavy unimok truck, driven by his nephew Freddie, a young Swiss visiting from Zurich. Fortunately, the unimok had a canvas top over the back. Karl and Freddie slept there while I curled up in the jeep. There are no hotels, or even a place to stay the night, in these small villages.

Next morning, we organized in a sea of black mud. With five small burros and two bony mules as pack animals, we began the trek up the slippery path. It had been worn smooth by the bare feet of natives who lived in small villages on the side of the Arushi Mountains.

About noon we came to a small clearing in the dense jungle of vines and trees. A small spring bubbled up from the spongy earth and trickled down the mountainside. It was the only flat spot I had seen since we started. We unloaded the gear and set up camp. There were two small rectangular tents for Karl and myself, and a larger round army tent for the boys. It was still misting; the damp, musty smell penetrated everything including our clothes. We built a fire, warmed up some canned food, ate and went to bed.

Next morning a heavy fog hung over the mountains. We didn't leave camp until 9 A.M. There was no benefit in departing sooner because we couldn't see 20 feet in that fog. When our sight improved we climbed about 2,000 feet to timberline and glassed the bush for nyala. The visibility was still poor, so when the rain began at about 4 o'clock, we came back to camp.

We saw two menelik bushbucks during the day, but I did not take one. We felt that the shot might spook the nyala. We would take the nyala first; it was by far the most important animal.

We saw tracks of nyala the next three days, but nothing else. The fog and rain stayed with us. Each day we were wet by the time we got back to camp.

On the fourth day we decided it was useless to hunt there any longer. Leaving the camp intact, we came down the mountain to the Danakil country in the Galla Desert. Karl knew of a small rest house owned by the railroad and operated by a Greek, where we could stay.

It was a filthy place, and the mosquitoes and giant bedbugs ate us alive. We had no other choice but to stay; it was a roof over our heads. Almost two years later, a doctor burned out two septic places on my legs that would not cure where those bedbugs had bitten me.

The Danakil area was named after the fierce nomadic tribesmen that lived in the territory. They travel constantly, the wives and children doing the work and minding the livestock while the men stalk food. They carry a long, smooth bore rifle and short dagger. Most men have bandoleers of cartridges criss-crossed over their shoulders, much like the banditos of

Mexico. They are a fierce and proud tribe and are often at odds with the government.

The country is flat and semi-desert covered by sparse vegetation. With the coming of the rains, however, the country becomes covered with thick grass on which the Danakil tribesmen graze their camels, sheep, burros and goats. The dry washes flood during the monsoon season, creating dense thickets two to three miles wide and many miles long. Here the lions will hide in the daytime and wait for the tribesmen's unsuspecting herds.

It was in one of these thickets that I shot my first lesser kudu. The beautiful little animal had eluded me on several safaris to Somali and the Tana River and Athi River in Kenya. It is an underrated animal, shy and elusive, and found in only a few African locations.

It was a stifling hot afternoon that Karl, I and the game scout (who must be with you at all times when hunting in Ethiopia) were picking our way through the dense brush following tracks of two kudu. Near sundown, the animals were feeding on the browse of the thicket. After leading us a long way into the thicket, they had separated. Then we began following the spoor of the male.

Suddenly there was movement. A dainty female was nibbling on a bush. We stopped and waited, watching her eat. Her big ears flicked forward, she turned her head and looked back. The bush separated and the bull walked into the small opening. I brought up my 300 Weatherby and shot him in the shoulder. He leaped forward one jump and collapsed.

We walked over to the beautiful male with the long spiral horns and measured them. They were 29½ inches. Karl shook my hand and said, "Congratulations." Then he added, "It will be dark very soon; I will go get the jeep." He left while I took out my skinning knife and began cleaning the animal.

When the job was completed, the game scout (who never carries a gun) and I sat down to wait. As usual on the desert at sundown, a warm breeze sprang up and rustled the dry leaves on the bush. Downwind there came a sound that always tingles the short hair on my neck — the grunt of a hunting lion.

The scout looked at me and said in his broken English, "Leon!"

I nodded, thinking of what I had heard and read about the lions of Ethiopia. They have lost their fear of humans after living with them over the centuries and being fed on their cows and camels.

Only in Ethiopia could you find a beisa oryx with a pair of horns like these.

The lion grunted again, this time closer. It was clear that he had smelled the scent of blood and was coming to investigate. The game scout stood up and moved about restlessly. He cocked his head to one side, listening for the jeep. Once again the lion grunted, very close now, and I stood up with my rifle. Then to one side, the bush rustled as a big body shook the dry leaves. Our eyes swung to the spot, but I didn't see the lion. Again there was movement, and it was obvious the lion was circling us. Then he growled and I knew he knew we were there. He was making up his mind how badly he wanted the meat. It was almost dark now; the next few minutes would be interesting.

But the decision was taken away from him by the sound of the jeep grinding through the bush to our right. I raised my gun and fired into the air. There was no landmark to guide Karl, and I knew he would not be able to find us without a fire or a signal. The jeep altered course and headed in our direction. Then Karl stopped the motor and called out. The scout answered and in a few minutes the jeep arrived.

We hunted four days in the open country of Danakil area. I took soemmerling gazelle, beisa, and oryx. "Lady Luck" smiled on me by giving me another world record animal — a lovely, little Phillips dik-dik with 3¼ inch horns, a full quarter inch longer than any other ever taken.

The trophy was an accident as most world records are. We were coming back to the rest house along a pathway when Karl stopped and said, "There is a dik-dik in that brush over there."

He was right. Through my binoculars I could see his horns rising high above the red tuft of hair on his head.

"Looks like a good one," I said. Karl agreed and I shot him. A few minutes later my tape showed it was a new world record.

After four days we went back to the mountains. We had allowed twenty days for this section of the safari and were back in the mountain camp on the eleventh day. The rain and fog had disappeared, and the sky was a brilliant blue. We again began climbing the mountains early each morning before sunup.

We tried everything for the next six days — early morning stalking, deep ravines, sitting at springs located deep in the dark jungle and glassing the high moorlands both morning and evening. We saw females, their young and an immature bull, but no trophy animals. The only reward was a fine record book menelik bushbuck.

On the seventeenth day I was sitting by a water hole with the game scout. Karl had left for business in Addis Ababa. About 10 A.M. the scout, who spoke little English said, "We won't find nyala here." I was surprised and asked why. He replied that there weren't any bulls in the mountains. They had been hunted too hard and would only come out at night. He guaranteed he could get me a nyala in three days. I told him that I would reward him well if he could do so. We immediately climbed down the mountain and began breaking camp. We also sent a runner to the village to intercept Karl. He arrived at 3 P.M. with our donkeys and mules. We loaded and were at the village by nightfall.

We loaded up and headed toward another range of mountains about 150 miles away that Karl thought to be a reserve. But the game scout assured him there was a small area not included in the restricted area. He was from the village and knew about it. We traveled all day and into the night over very bad roads. We were leading in the jeep and occasionally would get a short distance ahead of the big truck. We would then stop and wait until it caught up with us. On one stop, the truck did not appear. When we went back, we found the truck upside down in a ditch about 12 feet deep. No one was injured but some of the boys complained of sore backs, ribs and heads. We worked till early in the morning, trying to pull the truck out with the jeep's winch, but could not, even after building a platform of rocks by the beam of my flashlight. At 2 o'clock we gave up, laid down on the road and went to sleep. We were awakened at 6 A.M. by two huge log trucks on their way to a sawmill in the mountains. With the help of both trucks and cables, we brought the truck out on the road, reloaded it and continued on our way. The cab was smashed and the iron supports were bent, but it ran. Late in the afternoon, we limped into a village at the foot of the mountains. The game scout's relative came out to greet us as we set up camp near the edge of the village. We had two days left to hunt.

The first morning we climbed a steep mountain and hunted all day. We saw many fresh signs and heard sounds through the thick jungle, but did not see any animals. The second morning, with flashlight in hand, we started climbing another mountain at 4:30. It began to get light about 6:00. An hour later we saw wild heather above timberline. Only one small patch of bush remained and we would be out on top.

A local man and I were in front of the others by about 50 yards when we both saw a big bull nyala bolt to our left. I could hear the bull going through the bushes, but couldn't see him. The guide whistled urgently and I ran to his side. He pointed into the last few bushes at his end of the patch. I still couldn't see the animal; I could only wait. I knew the bull would have to make up his mind to do one of two things. He could run up into the open and over the top, or he could run across a narrow open space and head down in the jungle below. He could not stay where he was because the other men were coming into the bush at the lower end.

He made up his mind. I saw the huge lyre-shaped horns move through the bush toward the opening. He covered the open area in two mighty bounds, but my rifle moved with him as I squeezed off the shot. At the smack of the bullet, he turned towards us and away from the safety of the trees. With another mighty leap he sailed out into the open above the trees and plunged into the evergreens below. It was a spectacular sight. For a moment no one spoke, then everyone started yelling at once. Karl came running to slap me on the back. In a few minutes we had climbed down to where the big bull lay, magnificent in death — a trophy well worth working for.

The second half of the hunt started three days later when we arrived in the small town of Gambella—a sun-parched cluster of one-story shacks. Located on the banks of the Bora River, it borders the Sudan, about 1,100 miles due west of Addis Ababa. The store buildings, now in poor condition, had been built by the Italians during their occupation of Ethiopia in the thirties. There was no sign that any paint had been applied to them since the occupation. It was a filthy little village.

We were met by Peter Luthy, Karl's son, a good-looking young man about twenty years old. He had driven a jeep and trailer from Addis. It had taken him five days to do it, and he had overturned the jeep and trailer twice on the terrible roads. The windshield and top of the jeep had been demolished, the fenders and one side were caved in, but it ran. The iron trailer was another matter. We would have to repair it before going further.

We made arrangements for a place to sleep while Karl began welding the trailer and jeep back together, using a small portable welding outfit that worked off the motor of the jeep. Peter began getting dugouts (local canoes made from logs) together to build a raft. The Bora had no bridge or ferry, and there was no other way to cross.

Two days later, we were ready. The raft, constructed of five dugouts with poles lashed on top, was complete. We loaded up and crossed over without incident. We were now 150 miles from our destination, the Ghila River, where we hoped to find Nile lechwe and white-eared kob. The jeep had a heavy load. The all-metal trailer was piled high with our equipment, gasoline, oil and seven grown men. The road was bad. In fact, there was no road — just a trail. There was no shade, and the sun was so hot that you couldn't touch the metal on the jeep without burning your hand. Many

The only way to cross the Bora River was to construct a raft out of dugouts.

times the men jumped off to push us up a steep bank or pull logs and brush out of the path when we were in heavy timber.

We crossed two more small rivers, and it was lucky that we were in the dry season. The rivers had almost dried up. Only once did we come close to disaster when we hit a deep hole in the muddy water. But with everyone pushing, we got the jeep across without stalling. The water had run into the trailer and into the jeep. We hit a belt of hungry tsetse flies on two occasions.

The afternoon of the second day, we came to the Ghila River, a broad muddy stream which begins in the Ethiopian highlands and flows toward the Sudan. It disappears in a huge swamp where we hoped to take the Nile lechwe and white-eared kob. Just before we arrived at the river, a small airplane flew over us, going in the same direction. "There goes the prince," Karl said. When I inquired about it, he answered that Prince Abdorezza of Iran was going to be hunting in the same area. A camp had been set up by another outfitter, and the prince had flown down to join them.

We arrived at the river and ran into open hostility from one of the local men who came out from his mud hut. He informed us that we couldn't hunt there because it was the area of the other outfitter. We set up camp on the river anyway and waited to see what would happen. We didn't have a long wait. The next day the other outfitter, Tom Mattanovich, flew into Gambella and returned with an army major and the local police chief. He read an order from the governor prohibiting us to hunt in the area and ordered us to leave immediately. I was furious. I told both outfitters I wouldn't go and demanded two of Karl's men so I could cross the river to hunt. We were at a stalemate — I wouldn't leave and Karl couldn't hunt.

The next morning I was invited to visit the camp of Prince Abdorezza. This generous and fine sportsman invited me to hunt with him as his guest.

The hunt with Prince Abdorezza was not the usual, well-planned hunt for royalty with Persian rugs and silver service. We rode in a dilapidated unimok over some of the roughest country to be found. The prince absolutely forbid me to ride on top with the boys. He insisted that I sit in the seat with Tom Mattanovich while he sat on a truck tire, trying desperately to stay upright.

We covered about twenty miles along the river the first afternoon and never did get to the huge swamps of the Nile lechwe and white-eared kob. His Highness did shoot a very fine reed buck and roan after offering to let me shoot them first. I refused, saying I was his guest only when taking the two animals, the lechwe and kob. He made a fine shot on the reed buck, hitting him in the neck at about 150 yards.

The next morning we again got a late start because Tom insisted on pulling a Land Rover across the river at a shallow location and did not finish until noon. When he completed the job, the prince and I crossed the river and started for the swamps again.

We arrived late in the afternoon and were met by some local men with a dugout. It was late in the day, so the prince decided to stay at the Land

Young African boys play along the banks of the Bora River.

Rover parked on a high knoll overlooking the swamp.

As Tom was getting the dugout loaded, the prince and I looked over the swamps with our binoculars.

It was a tremendous expanse of low country. As far as I could see, what was once a sea of tall dead grass was now criss-crossed by narrow channels of dirty water. Most of the tall grass had been burned and what remained showed signs of damage by both man and beast. It was desolate land where thousands of crocodile lived in the sloughs. They dwelt in harmony with the beautiful black and white lechwe. Deep in the swamp I could see small herds

Watering cattle sometimes requires hauling buckets from deep wells.

of the antelope feeding, but they were too far away for me to judge the size of horns. Tom was ready to go so we got into the unstable, hollow log and pushed off for the opposite shore.

After landing we hurried out across the burned grass toward where the lechwe had been seen. The fine black ashes from the grass rose up from our feet in a cloud, clogging our nostrils and getting into our eyes. We crossed narrow fingers of shallow water that branched out from the larger canals and occasionally detoured when the water was too deep. It was near sundown when we reached the spot where I had seen the lechwe.

The area had been burned earlier, and new green grass had sprung up from the black ground. The lechwe were feeding on the new stubble. When we reached the spot, there were no lechwe in sight.

We headed for a large patch of tall grass not far away. Soon we were pushing our way through it.

Just as we came out the other side, the lechwe were going into another patch of grass about 200 yards away.

"Shoot the blackest one!" Tom ordered. I dropped down in a sitting position, resting my elbow on my left knee. I fired at the animal, killing him on the spot.

"I'm glad you killed him," Tom said. "It will be too dark to shoot in a few more minutes." We walked over to the antelope lying in the ashes. "We are lucky, he is a good one," Tom added.

By the time Tom had finished taking the cape and horns from the animal, it was dark. I was beginning to wonder how we were going to find our way back to the Land Rover without a flashlight.

The next three hours were about as tough as anyone could imagine. With the darkness came swarms of bloodthirsty mosquitoes who tried to devour us. The boys argued incessantly about which way to go. Several left our group and wandered off in the darkness, trying to find their way back.

We followed, guided by yells from one man, then another. We gave up trying to dodge the water; when we came to a canal, we just plunged in and waded across. It is still a wonder to me why someone did not fall prey to a crocodile that night. I believe it was only because of the noise the boys made by thrashing the water with their long wooden spears as we crossed.

After three hours of wandering around in that swamp, we saw the lights from the Land Rover shining in the darkness. It was one of the most welcome sights I had ever seen. It was a long ride back to the camp but a wonderful relief not to have the swarms of mosquitoes attacking us.

We finally got off to an early start the next morning. By the time the sun was coming up, we had crossed the river and were on our way down to the swamps again. It was a good thing too, because we were going to hunt white-eared kob. Their area was several miles beyond the point I had killed the lechwe.

We again parked at the same spot, but after crossing the large canal, we marched inland across the burned area at a steady pace.

When we came to several canals three to four feet deep, the boys went ahead thrashing the water and yelling. After three hours we reached a large plain that stretched in all directions, except for a solitary large tree now and then.

It was close to noon, so we had lunch under one of these trees. A mile away several herds of white-eared kob were grazing. The beautiful black animals with the white chest, belly and spots around the eyes made a lovely picture against the bright blue sky. In my opinion, these are the prettiest of all the gazelles or antelopes.

I finally killed two kob, one a very good one, and we made the long trek back to the Land Rover. When we arrived in the camp, I bid the prince good-bye and thanked him for his hospitality and generosity. During the three days I spent with Prince Abdorezza, I learned to respect and admire this fine hunter and gentleman. He is tough and dedicated. I understand why he is one of the very top hunters of the world, if not the top one.

Our small group once again made the long trip from the Ghila back toward Gambella. However, this time we stopped at a small place called Obobo and made camp on the river not too far from the village. We stayed there for another three days looking at elephant. I didn't find a good one, so we moved on to Gambella for our last three days of the safari.

Each morning we would cross the river very early from the village, take the jeep and drive back inland. I collected a very good waterbuck and Lelwel's hartebeest on the first day.

The second day we returned to Gambella to find two policemen waiting for us. Our rifles and trophies had been confiscated. Karl, Peter and the game scout were arrested and told to report in court the next morning. I gave Karl some money to post bail so he would not spend the night in jail. The next morning, the four of us — Karl, Peter, the game scout and I — appeared at the courthouse.

Court was being held in a ramshackle, one-story building with a circular screened porch. The scene was straight out of a storybook. The judge, a huge black man, sat at a scarred-up desk with a book opened before him. Across the room, by the door, a sergeant sat at a smaller desk with a book opened in front of him. The prisoners awaiting trial squatted or sat outside in the dirt in front of the building, guarded by three soldiers. Nearby, an old woman (nude to the waist, her head covered with dried blood) stood beating a tree with her fists and cursing the judge that had just sent her husband to jail. We sat down on a wooden bench and watched justice being meted out —Ethiopian style. A prisoner was brought in by a soldier. The prisoner bowed to his Honor, then stood facing him as the sergeant read from the book. When the judge spoke to the prisoner he replied by shaking or nodding his head. Then the judge read from the book again and passed sentence or fine. The soldier led the prisoner through the door and out of sight behind the building. Not more than ten minutes were spent on each case. The old woman's curses grew louder. The judge looked up and said something to the sergeant who called to the soldiers outside. One of them

Luckily I didn't have to give up this trophy or my guns to the Ethiopian government.

went over and threatened the old woman with his fist. Her mumbles died away, and I could again hear the loud buzzing of the flies passing in and out of the room through the screen that had rotted away.

When our turn came, the court machinery moved just as fast as in the other cases. We were charged (through an interpreter) of hunting in a forbidden area and failure to move when ordered. I protested and showed my government permits for the animals and area along with my hunting license. This was to no avail. The judge passed sentence — confiscation of guns and trophies, $1,000 fine for Karl Luthy plus $50 fine for the scout. I was furious and told his Honor, through the interpreter, that if this was a sample of Ethiopian justice, I felt sorry for the Ethiopians.

After we left I went to the governor's house and talked to him about the case. I pointed out that Ethiopia had suffered from a lot of adverse publicity in the past and this case would not look too good in print, where I felt sure I could put it. He agreed, and we both walked down the dusty street in the hot sun to the police station. He instructed the mayor (who jumped to quick attention) to release my guns and trophies and let Karl post bond, pending confirmation by the game department that we had permits and a license to hunt the area.

It was a face-saving gesture, and we both knew it, but all we were interested in was getting our gear and trophies freed and leaving.

The next morning at 11 o'clock, we boarded the DC-3 for Addis Ababa and the safety of the big city.

As I said in the beginning of this story, the Ethiopians have changed. They don't often kill white men these days — they just worry the hell out of them.

10

Tall tales in Angola

For years I delayed hunting Angola. I thought this was a country so full of game and so sparsely settled, that nothing could change its hunting conditions.

But suddenly there was a change, not from the Angolan natives but from terrorist groups from Zambia. They raided the local people, black and white, and any other visitors who happened to be in the area. This was a hit-and-run operation thought to be financed by Communist China.

From 1967 to 1971 the two best concessions, the Muccosso and Mavinga areas, were closed. The terrorists were doing their jobs well. Then the military discovered a way to combat the hit-and-run tactics of the raiding parties.

When an attack was made on a village or settler, the military moved in, but not with its usual combat men. They brought with them the small brown bushmen who had been trained in the use of firearms. These men were taken to the spot in helicopters and, like trained bloodhounds, took up the trail of the terrorists. Within a short time, moving at a fast trot, these small men could run down the larger Negro terrorists. The terrorist would feel the bullet before he realized the bushmen were anywhere nearby. It was a most

Opening pages: Angola proved to be the country to find the beautiful zebra, but we would soon learn that most game in the area had been over hunted by terrorists and ignorant visitors.
Opposite page: A regal leopard was the prize trophy taken in Angola.

effective method of controlling the terrorists and eventually discouraged the raiding parties that were operating in the hunting areas.

On August 1, 1971, Dr. Ed Chatwell and I arrived in Angola for a 37-day hunt. We had booked with Cunene Safaris, but this company dissolved just prior to our starting date, so Angola Safaris agreed to take over the safari.

Due to changing from one safari outfit to another, we did not know with whom we would be hunting. Ed and I did not care as long as the equipment was good and the area productive. We arrived in Luanda and were met by an agent of Angola Safaris who gave us our hunting and gun permits. We were then put on an airplane to Sa da Bandeira where very little English was spoken, but the agent assured us we would be met at the airport.

We were met, but not by English speaking people. We had a difficult time before we met a young Portuguese who had a pilot's license. He was out of a job after a disagreement with the superintendent of the oil company where he had been working. The hotels were full so we stayed the night with a Portuguese family. The next afternoon the young man flew us down to the desert camp near Mossamedes. By this time, both Ed and I were pretty well disgusted with the whole setup and eager to get going. We were told that the owner, Hernandi Espinha, was at the desert camp.

After getting lost twice and having to land to ask directions from natives, we finally found the camp and landed. It was a pretty hectic flight with an overcast sky and clouds blotting out the ground. I was glad to be on terra firma again.

Hernandi was an engaging fellow who smiled continuously. It was hard to stay angry with him very long. The quarters were comfortable and the food was good. After awhile, he was promising us the moon in his broken English — gemsbok, springbok, mountain zebra, leopard, dik-dik — any other special animals that I wanted. I am not really hard to please and if an outfitter can produce animals I want, he doesn't need to baby me.

Before it got dark, I set up a target and began to sight in the guns. I had a .300 Weatherby and .458 Browning. Ed had brought a .375 Winchester. I didn't have any trouble with the .300 Weatherby but the .458 gave me a problem when I started zeroing in with the four power scope that was mounted with a Griffin & Howe, slide on and off mount.

I only shot about five shells through Ed's .375 and it was on, but after five rounds with the .458 I still was not satisfied. I was getting a headache from the recoil.

Hernandi Espinha, owner of Angola Sararis, welcomes Ed Chatwell and myself to his country and promises us a good hunt.

The young Portuguese that had flown us down came out and asked if he could shoot my .300. I told him he could, but to be careful and not hold the scope too close to his face. I explained that on two occasions, once in India and again in Alaska, this gun had cut a man's forehead because it carried quite a wallop.

He assured me that he could shoot and fired a round hitting four inches from the bull at about two o'clock. I watched him and he seemed to know what he was doing. I fired the .458 again and stood aside so he could shoot. I laid down and didn't bother to watch him. The Weatherby roared and he grunted. I turned to look as blood began pouring down the gun and to the ground from the half moon cut in his forehead. He was really bleeding.

I took the gun from his hands, led him over to the dining room, called one of the boys and asked for some water and a clean cloth. I had him lay down while I pressed the edges of the cut together as best as I could to stop some of the bleeding. Then I took a band-aid and tried to patch the cut. The fourth band-aid finally stuck as some of the bleeding had stopped due to the cold, wet cloth we had been applying. I left him resting with another cold pad on his eye. He will always have a small half moon scar over his right eye. I call it the "Mark of the Weatherby Club."

Ed Chatwell is a dentist, not a medical doctor, so he seemed perfectly willing to let me handle the situation. He is a wonderful fellow and the most congenial hunting partner one could hope for. After a few more shots, all the guns were zeroed in. We had a fine dinner and called it a day.

The next morning Ed was paired with Antonio De Aguilar, a dashing young Portuguese who habitually drove with large black goggles and black gloves. I also found out from Ed that Antonio traveled at a very fast pace in his open Toyota.

I drew a very dour professional called Zecco, who spoke perhaps one word each hour, but he knew the country and the animals. That's all any hunter can expect.

That's the look of a happy hunter with a nice springbok.

The country was the usual African desert—sandy soil, sparse bush and short grass. In some areas there were low hills covered with an assortment of black volcanic rock. A few small springs were hidden at the base of these hills, but if you didn't know where they were located, you could die of thirst before finding one.

Small bunches of springbok were plentiful. I collected two that made the record book, shooting them at quite a long distance by African standards. Both shots were well over 250 yards. The small and lovely dik-dik (Damarland) were also abundant, hiding under almost every bush. I collected two of these little beauties that made the book.

The mountain zebra and Angolan gemsbok were proving to be very elusive. We saw only a handful of oryx and no zebra, even though two of the hidden springs had tracks of both species. Each time we visited the springs there were always fresh spoor.

The "Hartman," commonly called mountain zebra, is a fine trophy for any hunter. I had collected one in Southwest Africa on a hunt with Basie Maartens, but I wanted a second one for a rug in one of our bedrooms. They are by far the most beautiful of zebra with many long thin stripes in the coat.

The leopard that Hernandi had promised us was certainly there. I had never seen so many leopard signs. Each morning the sandy ruts of the roads were covered with fresh leopard tracks of all sizes. Zecco showed me a number of bait trees—small scrubby bush where they had baited leopards. Without exception, the trunk was scarred by the claws of leopards climbing the tree to feed. He also pointed out several trees where leopards had been killed.

We put out the springbok that I had killed, as bait. I planned to put out an oryx or zebra as soon as one was taken. Zecco said the desert leopard would feed on a quarter of zebra as quickly as on a small animal. I never question a professional in his area.

Hernandi had been guiding a group of Italian hunters, but after two days their hunt was complete. He offered to take me out for two days until the next clients arrived. I accepted and we hunted two days together.

Hernandi is one of those individuals who must be moving or doing something all the time. He is an excellent hunter and eager to get good trophies. A trophy hunter himself, he has several species listed in the record book.

We started out in the morning just at daylight and drove a long way south looking for gemsbok. About ten o'clock we sighted a small herd, but no good bull. We left them and continued looking as they galloped over the top of a rocky hill. We covered a lot of area. There were many springbok and a small herd of zebra that sighted us at the same time. They disappeared among the rock-strewn hills in a cloud of dust. They were real spooky.

We were coming back toward camp just before sunset. The round, red ball of the sun was touching the tops of the distant hills, causing one of the most beautiful sunsets I have ever seen. Hernandi suddenly said, "There's our gemsbok." They were there alright, standing on a small hill looking at us. A lovely line of tall thin horns were outlined against the red sky.

They turned and bolted away over the top of the hill. Hernandi threw the Toyota into second gear saying, "I will run around on the other side. Be ready." The Toyota plunged forward and Hernandi whipped it around the base of the hill. Not a gemsbok was in sight. "Funny," he said in his broken English, "They should be here."

I opened the door and got out as Hernandi followed. I ran forward and started climbing up the rock-strewn hill as fast as I could go.

It took me about ten minutes to near the top. I stopped for a minute to catch my breath. I peeked over the crest of the rocks and directly down into a bowl that held about thirty gemsbok, standing as silently as any group of animals I have ever seen.

I dropped back as Hernandi and I studied them through the binoculars for another minute; the light was going fast. "Number two from left," Hernandi whispered. I agreed with him mentally, raised the .300 and put a 180 grain bullet into the tan shoulder. The animal collapsed as the rest of the herd exploded and sailed back over the hill like a covey of quail.

"He's good," Hernandi grunted as we went forward cautiously. The gemsbok is a dangerous animal when still alive. He will charge anything and can be quite lethal. Some lions have found this out after being speared by the long horns. But this one was dead. His long horns, very thick at the base, measured 38-7/8 inches—a fine trophy.

Hernandi and I hunted two more days, and I took another gemsbok. He was not quite as good as the first, but a fine trophy, nevertheless. Yet the zebra eluded us. Zecco returned from his home, and he and I went out together for the next six days. We hung two more bait but each morning we checked them there was no sign they had been disturbed. It seemed

This gemsbok was shot just at sunset in Angola, his lovely horns outlined against the red sky.

impossible with so many leopards about, however, they just weren't feeding on bait.

I took a nice steinbok, shot about 1,000 feet of 16mm film of the lovely desert country, visited the great sand dunes to the south and got to know the area pretty well as we traveled many miles each day.

On the last day of the desert hunt, I shot a nice zebra stallion when we suprised a herd at a spring. They fled flat out toward their rocky home when I fired. It was a good shot, just behind the shoulder as the stallion cut across to join a few mares that had left the herd. He stopped after three or four lunges, reared straight up into the air and fell backward, dead by the time he hit the ground.

The desert had given me everything Hernandi had promised except a leopard, which surprised Hernandi most of all.

It took one day to fly into Sa da Bandeira, then to a camp in the Mavinga area. It is located near a great marsh south of the Muccusso region.

On the way through Sa da Bandeira, we picked up my hunter for this

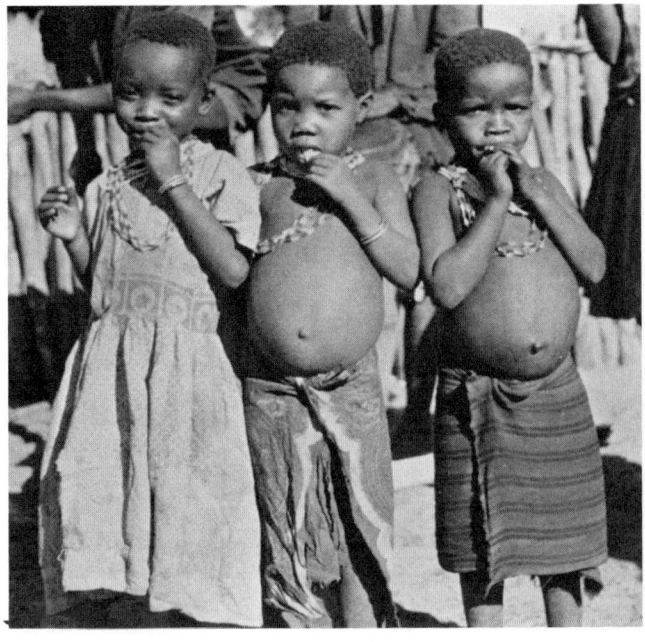

Above, a mountain zebra was taken, just as Hernandi had promised. At right, three young villagers face the camera with mixed reactions.

portion of the safari. He was Alfredo Feriera, a man who I came to know as one of the finest professionals in the business.

Alfredo is almost a legend in the bush country from Muccusso to the Cubango River, a distance of several hundred miles. Over the past thirty years, he has roamed this country at the request of the local people who have asked for help.

In one village, a lion or pride of lions were killing stock and people. In another village, a leopard had clawed a man who accidentally ventured too close to his kill. At other times, a bad buffalo or rogue elephant would be spreading terror among the natives. Alfredo answered all calls. He was the equivalent of all the game wardens in Kenya and other countries that have or had a game department. He shot the killer lion and leopard and drove the herds of buffalo and elephant from the shambas of the villages. He would do it alone and without pay. He answered the call for two reasons: his love for excitement and to help the helpless people.

I was continually amazed at the reception we received when we would drive into a small village hidden away in the bush to ask about game. He would simply say, "I am Alfredo."

The name Alfredo would be repeated by the people crowded around our car, and smiles would spread across their faces. We would be made welcome, assistance would be given and food and drink were offered. Although most of the villagers did not know him by sight, the stories of his prowess with a rifle had preceded him. I felt it was an honor to be traveling with such a fine hunter.

The camp was filled with four hunters and four professionals. Yet the hunting area was unlimited, without another camp within 100 miles. The flat land was covered by bush. It was divided by small rivers that caused vast marshes of tall papyrus and reeds. There were many species of animals in this area, including all of the big five. Even the rare situtunga and lechwe lived in the swamps.

I told Alfredo that I didn't particularly care to take a lion unless he was very good. He thought we had very little chance at a leopard. That didn't bother me. I had killed seven leopards, and unless one came easy and was a good male, I really didn't care.

Dr. Roche, a Frenchman from Paris was only interested in taking a good kudu, which he later did. The only man who wanted a lion was a newcomer to Africa, Sam Morse from Mississippi.

His hunter promised to get him a good lion. They chased one for five days, but finally gave up because the big lion was constantly on the move and wouldn't feed on their bait. One year later in the same camp, Morse's hunter was attacked by a big lion that had been wounded. He lost the use of his right arm as a result of being severely mauled by the lion.

Alfredo and I took good situtunga, red lechwe, Angola duiker, tsassaby, wildebeest, wild dog and roan before moving to the third and last camp of the safari on the Cubango River.

Something very interesting and unusual happened when I shot the roan and boys were skinning it out. I was watching the operation along with Alfredo, when a small brown bird perched on a branch directly above me. He jumped around and tweetered, acting very agitated.

"The honey bird is calling to you," Alfredo said.

"Is that what that is?" I answered.

"Yes, he wants to show you some honey."

"You're kidding," I said.

"No, no," Alfredo said, seriously. "He has found a honey tree."

Of course, I didn't believe him. I had heard of the honey bird many times while in Africa. I put these stories in the same bracket as the old wives' tales of long ago.

"How far do you think he would lead me?" I asked.

Alfredo shrugged, "Who knows?" he answered.

On the spur of the moment, I picked up my rifle which was leaning against a tree and said, "While they are caping out the roan, I will just see what this bird will do."

I walked off a few steps and the bird above me became even more agitated. He flew about 50 feet up an incline and again landed on a branch to begin his jumping and tweetering. I walked over underneath his tree and he immediately flew further up the incline to repeat his little dance.

And so it went, the bird leading and I following until the other men were out of sight among the trees. The bird finally picked a large branch instead of a small limb as he had been doing, and did a little dance on the limb, chirping up a storm. I looked closely at the tree and saw several bees fly out of a knothole in the branch. If I had not seen this, I wouldn't have believed it. He really had led me to a honey tree.

I stayed at the tree for a few minutes. Suddenly the bird flew away into the forest and was lost from sight. I returned to Alfredo and told him what had happened. He grinned widely and, in his amiable way, replied, "The honey bird likes you."

After cleaning out the roan and putting him into the Toyota, we returned to camp where we picked up two of the small bushmen. Alfredo told them about the honey tree. They were only too willing to return with us and try for the honey.

We stopped again at the spot where the roan had been skinned. Immediately the honey bird was back, chirping and dancing.

The bushmen took their axes out of the Toyota as I set up my tripod and 16mm camera to record the robbing of the honey tree.

We followed the bird up the hill and he again led us to the honey tree. The bushmen started a fire, then gathered some small branches covered with dark green leaves. They selected a double handful of dry grass and mixed it with the leaves.

They lighted the dry grass which, in turn, fired the green leaves and produced thick smoke. After tying a rope to the bundle, they climbed up the tree, looking like two brown monkeys with clothes on.

They held the smoke close to the opening in the limb, batting at a few bees that were buzzing around their heads. While one waved the smoke bundle around them, the other chopped the limb from the tree trunk. It came crashing to the ground. The bird had disappeared again. The two men climbed down from the tree; and while one waved the smoke maker about, the other neatly chopped open the limb to expose several rows of honeycomb filled with the thick, golden liquid. They proceeded to pry out the honeycomb with their hands and put it in a container. One of the bushmen carefully placed a small piece of comb filled with honey on the top of the limb and moved away. The honey bird appeared suddenly, perched above us and just sat there. "Well, I'll be damned," I said.

Alfredo smiled again. "He is waiting for his part," he said.

We walked away, following the bushmen. Alfredo explained to me that the honey bird must always get his share, or next time he would lead you to a big snake or a lion. He was dead serious so I didn't argue the point. After all, I had witnessed a strange thing that day.

Two days later, we left the camp and traveled 150 miles south to our third destination. It would be our last stop on the Cubango River. We planned to camp out that night and took some bedding with us. We drove until sundown and were just about to make camp for the night when Alfredo suddenly jammed on the brakes and said, "Wild dog, wild dog." He seldom showed so much emotion. Then I saw them. A group of five dogs were coming down a small ravine where a duiker had just rushed out at full speed.

"Shoot them, shoot them," Alfredo urged. "They are bad. Shoot them."

Without thinking, I raised my rifle and killed the first one, then the second, a third and crippled a fourth with my last shell.

"Good, good," Alfredo said jumping out of the Toyota, "Let's find the cripple."

I was putting shells into the magazine and feeling sorry about shooting the four animals. I had only killed one other wild dog before in my life. I don't enjoy killing animals without a reason, and never have.

Alfredo sensed my hesitation. "You should not feel sorry," he said. "These animals will kill everything in this area, and eat some almost alive. They are bad." I had never heard him speak like this before. He really hated these wild dogs. I followed him and within 50 yards saw the wounded animal on the ground. As he staggered to his feet, I shot him again, killing him instantly.

"I want the hide of one," I said. "I never have killed anything and just let it lay."

Alfredo nodded. In the twilight the two gunbearers did a fast job of ripping the skin off, taking the head and skull intact. While they completed the job, I heard an odd musical sound from the side of the hill.

"He is calling for his brothers," Alfredo said, his teeth gleaming in the semidarkness. Again the call sounded as I unhappily walked back to the car. Alfredo was probably right, but I mentally resolved to never pile up several of the same species again without a better reason.

The next day we drove into the Cubano camp. It was a very comfortable place indeed. The pleasant camp was located right on the south bank of the river.

I wanted a hippo for a head mount. The first thing Alfredo and I did was walk down the river about a mile, and I shot a big bull in the skull. After his head had bubbled below the water, we walked back to camp, leaving the two boys to keep an eye on the dead animals. We had lunch, then sat around for a few hours. We were still resting when one of the boys came running into camp to tell us the hippo had surfaced.

This bushman chief still uses the primitive bow and arrow to catch his game.

Sure enough, the huge body had swelled larger with gas and was floating like a huge cork in the center of the river. The natives from the village across the river from our camp were waiting in two log dugouts.

A lot of palaver and thirty minutes later, the men in the dugouts tied ropes to the huge body and started towing it down the river. However, after a few yards, three other hippo surfaced very close to the body of the dead animal and the men. They made a hasty retreat back to the far bank. They wouldn't go out into the river again, even after I fired a shot into the water close to the floating body to frighten the other hippo away. I don't blame the men for staying out of the water because the other animals kept disappearing, then popping up again close to the dead hippo despite my shots to keep them away. Alfredo explained that the hippo was slowly drifting over a hippo pool where they all lived, and the animals would not leave. We watched as the body slowly drifted down to a small island in the river, where women and children from the village had gathered. They had rowed over in another boat to await the floating meat market.

It was nearly dark when the hippo reached the island. The slow journey made it too late for the butchering. Alfredo had told them we wanted the headskin and they must remove it in order to have the meat. As we left he forbid them to start cutting the hippo until morning. Knowing they had not brought anything to sleep on, I wondered how they would spend the night. The crowd was predominantly women and children, some of them quite young in age. They would have to lie on a rock or the ground if they wanted to sleep. There was no other choice. I thought to myself that some of the back-to-nature nuts I have met should have to make such a tough choice a few times. Then they would begin to love shoes and appreciate the everyday comforts they had taken for granted.

The next morning when the sun came up, we again returned to the river where the natives waited patiently for the meat. After tying ropes to all four legs, the entire crowd began dragging the body to shore. The 5,000 pound beast was towed to the edge of the river and the headskin removed.

Then the butchering really began. Not a scrap of meat was left on any bones when the process was completed. Most of the smaller bones disappeared into the huge woven baskets carried on the heads of the women. They formed a continuous line that flowed from the island to the north shore and disappeared into the bush. Nothing went to waste, not even most of the intestines.

Two days later we visited the village as honored guests. We were even invited to the voodoo and witchcraft enclosure, where grotesque masks and fish net costumes decorated with animal hair and other talismans were made. It was a very interesting place not often seen by a white man.

I was also shown the circumcision post where the young boys passing into manhood were tied while the ceremony was performed. Two of the youngsters painted black, white and red for the occasion, slunk away as we came out of the enclosure of wooden stakes and brush.

It would be ten days before they would be allowed to return to their respective mud and stick huts. A wild celebration would follow, with plenty of pombe. Many nights that followed I was awakened from time to time by singing and the beating of drums.

Another structure had been built a short distance from the painted and notched post where the boys were to be tied. The simple hut was composed of six posts which supported a framework about five feet above the ground. The thatched roof was woven of branches and leaves to keep out the hot sun. Here the mothers of the boys were forced to stay until the circumcision rites were over. They were not allowed to sleep or even return to their homes.

These were the tribes of primitive Africa, not the partly civilized natives that live in Kenya and Uganda. These people had not changed much in centuries.

However, even as primitive as these blacks are, the bushmen live on even a lower scale. He is nearly always dependent on other people for the necessities of life. He earns his food by tending the cattle of the Negro and does most any other job delegated to him. As a rule, the black man has not been too generous and benevolent toward his smaller fellowman. When the going gets too tough, the bushman picks up his bow and poison arrows, collects his wife and children, and disappears into the bush.

His needs are very minimal. He has no permanent shelter. His crude protection could not be classified as a house. He simply sticks some branches into the ground, pulls them together at the top and covers it with leaves to keep out some of the sun. He crawls into this pitiful shelter only when necessary, as it is seldom more than three feet high.

After awhile, either the bushmen who leave an area will return, or some other wandering tribe will stop, and the relation between the Negro and bushmen will resume. Both, perhaps, are better for the separation.

A few days after I took the hippo, I shot an elephant in very much the same manner. I also had another unusual experience with this (my eighth) elephant. We had come up on a herd of elephants after four to five hours of tracking in the hottest portion of the day. They were dozing under several trees scattered over a wide area. This, of course, is always "sticky," as the British professional would say. The Angolan elephants are considered dangerous because they are inclined to be much more violent and ill-tempered than their cousins in East Africa. I don't know why it is, but this is also the case with several species of animals; they are quite docile in one area and touchy in another.

A good example are the lions of Kenya. They are pretty much pussycats compared to those in Botswana who will charge without much provocation. If you rile him he will definitely come for you. Quite a few people have been mauled by lions in Botswana, but such attacks are seldom seen in Kenya.

It is quite the opposite with the African buffalo. In Kenya he is a fierce animal. If he is threatened he will charge at the least provocation. But in Botswana I have seen buffalo herded by a Land Rover like a bunch of cattle. There is very little spirit in the huge brute.

In Angola the elephants are mean as hell. You don't sneak into the center of a herd to look them over if you are in your right mind. It's a good way to commit suicide.

Alfredo, while known to be a fearless man, had great respect for

The game of Angola — we were fortunate to find such a fine collection. Opposite page, a waterbuck and a western situtunga. At left, a delicate oribi and below, a good tessebe.

elephant. He would not take chances with them. I found that out early when I saw three cows actually seeking us out after they winded us. I was convinced that the stories of elephants killing a number of people in Angola were true.

So we came upon a herd and used extreme caution before making any sudden moves. We wanted to look them over to find the best animal. However, instead of sneaking among them as we would have done in East Africa, we chose a safer method. Alfredo climbed a tree while one of the boys climbed another. After a short time, both climbed down. The boy came over and held a brief chat with Alfredo. We circled around and they repeated their earlier action.

This time after the talk, we moved forward behind two large fallen logs. Through the bushes directly ahead, not more than 75 yards away, I could see three elephants standing under a tree. By looking to both right and left, I could distinguish the dirty grey shapes of others under other trees.

"There is the best one," Alfredo whispered, pointing to a bull under the nearest tree. I maneuvered around until I saw the tusks, but was not too impressed by the size. The elephants in Angola are noted for their huge bodies (world record, 13 feet, 2 inches at the shoulder), rather than their ivory.

He looked to be about a 55 to 60 pounder. I had not seen anything better so I resigned myself to shooting him.

I stepped away from the shelter of the tree trunks and centered the cross hairs of the .458 on his right shoulder, low and a bit back. I was just squeezing the trigger when suddenly he just flopped down.

I mean that literally — he just flopped down. He didn't kneel, either on front or back knees, or give any indication that he was going to lie down; he just relaxed and fell to the ground. He landed on his side with his back to me. I looked at Alfredo in bewilderment, as I had never seen an elephant lie down like that.

Alfredo smiled and shrugged his shoulders, the Portuguese gesture for saying, "That's the way it goes sometimes."

"What now?" I whispered as the two cows wandered off to join the others. The bull had almost flopped down on them and probably had disturbed their siesta. "Shoot him in the back," Alfredo suggested, "then kill him when he raises up." I nodded and again trained the rifle on the great grey body, half hoping to hit his backbone.

At the crack of the Browning, all hell broke loose as the cows started trumpeting and milling about. The bull raised his front feet, preparing to lift himself. Just before he raised up, I fired into his shoulder and he flopped down again, dead.

By that time, a few of the cows had decided where we were and came charging for us. We beat a hasty retreat, running downwind until they lost us.

A short time later we returned and looked the bull over. He was a huge animal in body size. He measured 11 feet, 1 inch at the shoulder, and his overall length was 25 feet 7 inches. There was little doubt we had taken a very large specimen. I told Alfredo that I wanted the headskin for a head and shoulder mount. We went back to the river across from the village to spread the good news that meat was available.

When we reached the bank of the river, Alfredo called across to some girls who were filling buckets and jugs with water. Within a minute or two, they all scrambled up the banks screaming at the tops of their lungs and running toward the village.

It wasn't long before a line of people came streaming out of the village toward a landing where several dugouts were beached. Men, women, children and dogs came, all caught up in the excitement of having enough meat to fill their bellies, an event which does not happen often in this country. Some of the more reckless young men plunged into the river, holding large knives in their mouths, and swam across. I wouldn't have done that for 10,000 dollars. I had seen a few very large crocodiles in that river.

The first of the young men reached the shore and came over to the Toyota, his face split by a happy-go-lucky grin. He was a magnificent specimen of a man, about six feet tall with wide, bare shoulders and a slim waist. He was shortly joined by others. Alfredo pointed in the direction where the dead elephant lay and gave them landmarks to follow. They immediately departed in that direction.

The long line of people and dogs continued to cross the river after the first young men, in the rays of the late afternoon sun. I was reminded of a long line of ants converging on a dead beetle. I had seen the sight many times. I knew from experience that the final results would be the same.

The huge carcass of the elephant would disappear into the buckets, baskets and stomachs of these hungry people. They had agreed to save the

This was a fine roan taken in the Cubango area.

headskin and ivory for us.

The next morning we went out early as usual for our morning hunt. It was almost two o'clock when we arrived at the place where I had killed the elephant.

It was a fantastic sight to see. Every low bush and branch of the trees was completely covered with strips of meat. People were cooking small pieces under several trees. The huge carcass had disappeared. Only a few of the larger bones remained. The head and pelvic bones were lying in a huge puddle of blood, amid the half-digested foliage from the stomach and intestines. Even the fat had been trimmed from the intestines; the huge stomach lining was split open and spread out over a rack to dry. Nothing was going to waste.

The rest of the hunt in Angola was uneventful except the incident of Sam Morse's leopard, which was unusual. Sam Morse had finally killed the leopard that he wanted so badly. He shot it just below camp on the river where the small airstrip had been cleared and leveled. It was surrounded by grass about three or four feet high; a few low bushes grew along the river bank.

They were returning to camp at sunset when they saw two leopard near the edge of the airstrip. Sam shot one and the other disappeared into the thick and tall grass. He shot a large female about six feet long with beautiful dark skin. Sam was very pleased that he had the opportunity to take a leopard. We sat around the fire that night talking about leopards, and Alfredo had a story of his own.

A few years ago, deep in the interior of Angola in the Muccusso district, Alfredo ran a small trading shop. One day he was notified that a large leopard was raiding a village and stealing goats at night. He was too busy at the time and told the villagers they must wait a week before he could come and kill the cat.

But the villagers held a meeting and decided that they would bait the leopard. One of them who owned an old smooth bore musket would sit in a tree above the bait and shoot the leopard. And so it was arranged over the protest of the man who was to shoot the leopard, as he was not quite certain of the results.

They tied a goat at the edge of a large swamp where the leopard lived. The man got into the tree above the bait about twenty feet off the ground. The sun sank lower over the swamp and the villagers departed. The lonely goat started crying out. The cries continued for fifteen minutes before a large male leopard parted the tall reeds and came charging out. He killed the goat instantly by grabbing him by the throat. As he lay on his belly holding the goat by the neck, the man above fired the muzzle loader and lost his balance. In order to keep from falling out of the tree, he dropped the gun. I now tell the balance of the story as Alfredo told it beside the campfire in Angola.

"The shot broke the leopard down in the back legs," Alfredo told us in his broken English. "The leopard was growling and rolling over. He looked up, saw the man in the tree and said, 'Oh, so you are the one who shoots me; I will chew on you!' So the leopard crawled and, not having the use of his hind legs, climbed the tree with only his front legs. The man on the first limb started kicking and yelling when the cat gets to him. But the leopard grabs a foot and chews on it for awhile. Then he is tired because he cannot hold so long with his front legs. So he backs down to the ground to rest." Alfredo paused while we all leaned forward to hear the rest of the story. He was a master at storytelling and enjoyed it as much as we did.

"After he rest," he continued, "the leopard slowly climbed up the tree again and chewed on the screaming man. The villagers are afraid to come. Three times this cat climbed the tree" Alfredo said, "and chewed on the man, then he is too tired to chew anymore and returns to the swamp."

"The man comes down with chewed feet and goes to the village. They send a man for me and I come and kill leopard." Alfredo ended his story and looked around the circle of listeners with a grin on his face.

Later, when the group around the fire broke up and we were on our way to our respective tents, Sam asked me, "Do you really think a leopard could move that well on just his front legs?"

"A leopard, Sam, is the strongest and most agile cat in the world. I wouldn't doubt Alfredo's story at all," I said.

I would have reason to remember that statement the very next night.

The birds were just beginning their morning chirping, when the zipper to my tent slid down softly. Alfredo stood in the opening, crooking his finger at me while putting a finger to his lips for silence. I rolled out, pulled on my pants, stepped into my tennis shoes and followed him silently into the early dawn. Not a soul was stirring.

We went down toward the landing strip, stopping at the skinning hut and rack on the edge of the circle of tents that made up the camp.

The smell of drying hides and meat was strong in the early morning air. Alfredo and I stopped at the rack where some of the skulls and horns were placed to dry. Reaching under the rack, he pulled out a mutilated carcass of what I recognized immediately as a leopard.

However, there was quite a bit missing. A large hole was in the side and one ham was gone. "What happened?" I asked.

"The beeg father came and ate his wife," Alfredo said, smiling.

"You mean the male came into camp last night and ate part of the female?"

He nodded, "Come, I show you the tracks."

We went down toward the river where the road led to the airstrip and, sure enough, there were the pug marks of a large leopard coming into the

Alfredo Ferrera, the famed professional hunter of Angola, helped me in taking my eighth leopard.

camp and going back toward the airstrip. We followed them to the strip about 500 yards away. I was surprised to find the dusty flat area covered with leopard tracks. Alfredo was examining one area and I another.

"Alfredo," I called, "Here are both of their tracks, male and female."

He held up three fingers and said simply, "Three." I crossed over to where he stood. There in the dusty earth were three sets of tracks—the unmistakable large pug marks of the male, the smaller tracks of the female and a third set of tiny tracks.

"Baby," Alfredo said.

"A family, what do we do now?" I asked.

"We kill the beeg male," Alfredo said.

"That will leave the young one alone," I protested.

"Is better," he answered. "If beeg male get hungry he will eat the little one without the mother."

"Do you think he is old enough to survive?"

"He will do alright," Alfredo said with conviction. "He eat mice, bird and small animals. Is better that we kill the male."

We went back to the camp and got a half of an impala that was hanging in the cooking area. Then we collected the carcass of the leopard and took both down to the far end of the airstrip.

We made a drag with the carcass of the leopard over the landing strip area along the river and back to the stunted tree on the riverbank, 75 yards from an anthill. The boys hung the impala in the tree and put the leopard carcass at the base.

"The leopard will feed on the meat at the base and not go up the tree to the bait," I protested to Alfredo.

"We will cover it with thorn bushes," he answered.

"He will get it anyway," I said. After shooting seven leopard and seeing their habits for over fifteen years all over Africa, I knew leopard pretty well.

But they left the carcass there, covering it with thorn brush. We were hunting until an hour before sunset. After leaving the Toyota in camp, we walked down to our blind that the boys had made on top of the anthill. I was surprised that Alfredo didn't carry any gun at all. I am always more comfortable with a shotgun handy when dealing with a leopard. Later on, I discovered that there was no shotgun in the camp.

The sun dropped down and twilight came on fast. Down below the tree, the shadows thickened. Suddenly we both heard it at the same time — the crunching sound of a leopard eating. He had gone for the carcass under the tree. By moving just a bit, I could see his hindquarters but not the complete body, as he stood chewing on the carcass. In a way, it disturbed me to see the leopard feeding on his mate. I waited with the cross hairs centered just in front of his hips, hoping that he would pull back from the bush and I could shoot him in the shoulders. I had killed seven leopards prior to this one with a single shot.

It grew darker, the light fading badly, when he suddenly pulled back and straightened up. I started to squeeze the trigger when he stepped forward again, just as the shell exploded. There was a savage snarl and a lot of action behind the tree in the bush.

"Where did you hit him?" Alfredo whispered.

"Not too good," I answered.

"Too far back. We will wait," he said. It grew darker and there was no sound. He pulled out a flashlight and said softly, "Let's go down." If there was ever a time that I didn't want to go, it was then, but what can you do? Pride is a strange thing. I would have gone if there were two wounded leopards.

However, much to my relief, he meant let's go down and back to the camp, which we did. There we asked Antonio, Alfredo's brother, to drive our Toyota while Alfredo got a big powerful flashlight.

We drove back to the landing strip. Alfredo and I stood up in the Toyota while he directed the light into the tall grass, and I held my rifle ready.

He was still a distance from the tree when Antonia began to drive very slowly, crisscrossing the area. We were about 25 yards from the tree when the light swept near the river and landed on two eyes, shining like a pair of emeralds. They stared at us for a second, then disappeared. Alfredo swept the area with his light again. A spotted figure, blending almost perfectly with the dry, brown grass, disappeared. "His hind legs are dead," Alfredo said, and I remembered his story.

We found the wounded cat three more times, and each time I shot and missed as he blended with the grass. He had moved more than 300 yards from where I had first shot him, dragging his hindquarters.

Once more we found him, but this time he was tired of running. He came for the Toyota, snarling savagely as his powerful front legs pulled him forward. He was an awe inspiring sight of ferocity as I shot him in the top of the shoulders. He collapsed about 30 feet from the Toyota.

Alfredo gave the light to Antonio to hold on the cat while he climbed out of the Toyota, got a stick, then climbed back into the car and threw it at the animal. He didn't move. After a few moments Antonio backed the Toyota around and turned the headlights on the leopard. I approached him carefully, touching him with the end of the gun barrel. He still didn't move. He was dead.

I was truly convinced that Alfredo's story of the leopard climbing the tree and chewing the man's leg was true. Without a doubt, pound for pound, they are the most powerful cats in the world and the most vicious when aroused.

11

Breaking records in Southwest Africa

One beautiful June day I arrived in Windhoek, southwest Africa, to go on safari with Basie Maartens. This was to be a short hunt for special animals found in southwest Africa, especially the rare mountain zebra.

I was also very interested in hunting the Kalahari Desert for the magnificent gemsbok, the largest of all the oryx. The bull of this species weighs between 400 and 500 pounds. The world record on length of horn is 48 inches, established by a bushman sometime in the last 100 years.

I also planned to hunt the small and lovely springbok, one of the most plentiful animals in southwest Africa. A strange characteristic of this animal is that when fatally wounded, the brown hair on top of his rump parts and shows the almost pure white, short body hair underneath in a four-to-five-inch white fan. This muscular reaction lasts only a few minutes, then the long brown hair relaxes and closes back together, hiding the white hair underneath.

The fourth animal I wanted to add to my collection from this area was the Cape hartebeest. The hartebeest, like the other animals of this species has

Opening pages: A herd of bontebok cross through the grassy plains of Southwest Africa. Opposite page: A beautiful gemsbok with a remarkable set of horns was one of the prize trophies taken in Southwest Africa.

very crooked horns. But unlike the others that are a dull tan, the Cape hartebeest has a beautiful dark red coat.

Dr. Ed Chatwell was another hunting companion on this trip. He was also interested in adding these same animals to his collection.

Basie met us at the airport and, without going into the city, drove us out to the first hunting area. Rea, his charming wife, and Freddie Schmidt, the other professional hunter, had already set up camp.

Hunting was limited to three days in the first area, located 125 miles northeast of Windhoek on a 16,000-acre ranch. The owner ran 900 head of cattle on the beautiful, level country, covered with lush grass that grew about 18 inches high. Scattered bush covered several acres. It was ideal for any type of grazing animal.

The first days of hunting resulted in a good Cape hartebeest and springbok.

We changed into our hunting clothes and went out to look over the game. Several herds of hartebeest and springbok were spotted along with a few ostrich. Late in the afternoon we saw a herd of kudu bulls. They were young bulls, big in body, but the largest would measure less than 30 inches of horn, a long way from the 42 inches required to make the record book. They still made a lovely sight so I photographed the herd as they milled about, then broke for the thick bush and safety.

We returned to camp at sundown without taking any trophies; that would come later. The first night in camp was cold, and by morning there was ice on the edge of the small pond near our campsite. The sky was a brilliant blue with little or no wind.

Basie and I were off before sunup and spotting springbok and hartebeest immediately. We drove for three hours looking over the herds before making a decision on the animal with the best set of horns. Before noon I shot a bull hartebeest with horns that measured over 20 inches. He was a good animal that made the book with an inch to spare, but we felt we could do better.

The second day of hunting produced a 23½-inch Cape hartebeest and a 13-inch springbok. We felt good about the hartebeest as he would place about twentieth in the record book. The springbok was a good buck at 13 inches, but we were shooting for the book on all species.

On the third day, I took another springbok that measured 14½ inches. The animal also made the record book, as the minimum is 14 inches. I saw many ostrich and could have taken a pair but did not do so. The same day I saw another herd of greater kudu, composed of four cows and a magnificent bull. I was tempted to take the bull but felt he was not better than the animal I found in Mozambique. I photographed the group with my 16mm camera until the bull sailed over a five-foot fence and raced into the thick bushes after the cows.

The fourth morning we broke camp and left the ranch. Basie, Dr. Ed Chatwell and I headed for the Namib Desert area located on the west coast of southwest Africa near the Diamond Belt. It was here we expected to find the rare mountain zebra.

The area is 130 miles southwest of Windhoek. The gravel road wound through a range of hills that rose to a height of 7,500 feet. The low mountains were barren of trees; some were covered with coarse bunches of grass. We saw very little game during the four-hour drive, only a few springbok and steinbok. We arrived at the ranch house at sunset.

The ranch, owned by Mr. Richder, sets on 70,000 acres of rolling hills that fade into the Namib Desert, the most arid and desolate land in southern Africa. In addition to cattle, Richder raises several thousand head of Caracul sheep on the ranch.

In the hills bordering the desert live the mountain zebra, the most rare and beautiful of the species.

Shooting a zebra is not difficult, and this hunt was no exception. By 9:30 the next morning Ed and I had our mountain zebras.

We came upon the herd as they emerged from a valley in the low hills. Two shots brought down the zebra. The hunt was over, and we looked forward to having two beautiful rugs on our trophy room floors.

The zebra was also prevalent in Southwest Africa, and was an easy animal to take.

By late afternoon the skins were salted down, packed away, and we were on the road again. Heading southeast, we were on our way to gemsbok country. In fact, we would be hunting on a ranch separated from the Gemsbok National Park by an eight-foot wire fence.

This ranch is owned by Mr. A. Hanzel and covers about 36,000 acres. Hanzel proved to be a hard-fisted, clear-eyed strong pioneer — the kind of man needed to settle a hard land like southwest Africa. This he had successfully done. He was about 65 years old and could retire anytime, move to Capetown or Johannsburg, and live out his remaining years in luxury. He preferred to live on the land he had conquered.

He visited us the first night in camp. We sat around the campfire until late, talking about the old days when lion made his life exciting but miserable by killing his sheep and cattle.

Morning dawned clear and cold as we began across the sand dunes of the Kalahari Desert. Most dunes were covered with grass, but now and then, the bright red sand of a bare dune would sparkle in the morning sun.

We immediately saw gemsbok in herds of five to thirty. We checked closely for good heads, but did not find what we wanted and returned to camp without taking an animal.

My first gemsbok fell short, but this second animal was considered the best ever seen in Kalahari. Its 45-inch horns well surpassed the record book minimum.

The second day was much like the first. We drove all day, spotting many gemsbok, a few springbok and two hartebeest. We also saw a lone cow eland that had attached itself to a herd of gemsbok. When the gemsbok took flight, the eland went with them.

We returned to camp after dark again without taking a gemsbok.

Finally on the third day I took a magnificent bull with horns that measured over 41 inches. They were huge at the base, and Basie and I thought he would measure over 42 inches, the minimum to make the record book, but he didn't. We could hardly believe the tape as the bull was without a doubt, the best we had seen. We returned to camp pleased with the magnificent bull, but somewhat dismayed with the prospect of getting one high in the record book.

The rare bontebok almost disappeared in the nineteenth century, but is now protected in a number of preserves.

Rowland Wards' Records of Big Game of Africa confirmed that few gemsbok grew horns in excess of 42 inches, and most of them were taken many years ago. The minimum, in my opinion, is two inches higher than it should be, but all a confirmed trophy hunter can do is keep trying. The limit on gemsbok was two; we still had one to go.

Near the end of the fourth day we had looked at five to six hundred gemsbok and still had not found one that we were sure would make the book. Then, late in the afternoon, we came upon a herd of about thirty animals grazing near a huge, barren dune of red Kalahari sand.

Basie and I glassed the herd closely and he said, "Check that third female from the right."

"You mean the small one with the big horns?" I asked.

The delicate impala was another fine trophy taken in Southwest Africa.

He nodded. "That's the one," he said. "If she won't make it we may as well give up. We could go on like this for the next ten days and never know."

"What bothers me is that she is so small in body," I said. "That may make the horns seem longer."

We studied the animal a bit longer and he again said, "That's the one." So I shot her, and the rest of the herd fled over the dune, leaving her lying on the red sand.

We measured the horns in silence. I momentarily forgot the usual remorse I always feel when I take a beautiful animal for my collection as the inches on the tape grew and grew 41, 42, 43, 44, 45 and over. Basie stood up and hit me on the back with the flat of his hand, almost knocking me down. "We've done it," he shouted. "Over 45 inches — the best that's ever been taken in this part of the Kalahari." The long straight horns were beautiful in the waning rays of the late evening sunlight. I felt very pleased and proud of the set of lovely horns from the red sands of the Kalahari Desert that would grace the walls of my trophy room.

The last leg of our safari was the long trip to Grahamstown, South Africa to take a bontebok, one of the rarest of African game and one that has been protected by the government for over forty years.

Basie, Ed and I drove down in the Land Rover. It was a long, hot ride and I was very pleased when we arrived at "Yellow-woods," the ranch where we would hunt.

I found Freida and Bobby Millar to be two of the nicest and most gracious people I had ever met. They owned "Yellow-woods," and once we arrived, the place was ours.

He was a huge man, weighing well over 300 pounds with a voice to match. His clear, blue eyes sparkled when he talked. For all his weight, he still enjoyed life. She was a gracious hostess, and once inside their rambling old ranch house, anyone was assured he would be a well-fed and comfortable guest.

After dinner we sat before the fire, telling stories of hunting and the settling of South Africa. Bobby's forefathers were early settlers when the country was young.

Next morning we drove down to the large paddocks of pastures, as they are called in the States, to look at the bontebok, a beautiful, rare antelope. Five different colors ranging from black to white softly blend together, making it one of the most beautiful of all antelopes.

The animal had suffered the same fate as the American buffalo or bison that roamed our central and western plains by the millions. The herds were shot by professional hunters for commercial purposes during the nineteenth century until they almost disappeared from the earth.

The bontebok was shot by the early South African settlers, as was the American bison for its skin and meat. Finally, only a small remnant of less than a hundred remained. But unlike the bison, which was saved by a private party, this small herd was put into a bontebok preserve on the tip of Good Hope near Capetown where it flourished.

No licenses were issued for a period of almost fifty years. In 1964 I had the good fortune of getting the first one. A second permit went to Nicolas Franco, Jr., of Spain, but he was involved in an automobile accident shortly thereafter, making my license the only one filled that year.

In one paddock, Bobby had five bulls on pasture all about the same age and about the same size in horn length. We studied them through binoculars for over an hour; then we visited the other paddock where the main herd grazed. There were about forty-five to fifty animals in this herd, most of them female. The head bull was larger in body size than the five bulls in the other paddock. His horns were, without a doubt, heavier at the base. However, he had worn them down until they could have been a fraction shorter than those of the younger bulls.

Bobby told us that he had to separate the mature bulls or the old herd bull would kill them. He had already killed two young bulls and a female, not long before I had arrived.

It was hard to believe such a lovely and delicate animal could be so aggressive. Then I remembered seeing a small duiker, not much heavier than a large jackrabbit, fight ferociously in the dense jungle in Kenya and in the Abaderes. Often the fight would end in the death of one of the animals. Once when hunting bongo with Tony Seth-Smith, two duiker had run almost between his legs as we stalked our prey. Both were so engrossed with strong emotions — one to escape and the other to kill his rival — that both ignored us. They disappeared into the bush while we watched in silence.

It was very difficult to judge which one of the bulls had the best horns. I couldn't make up my mind so I told Basie I would sleep on it.

Next morning I again looked at both herds and made up my mind. It was

In discussing fine tropies of horned game, one cannot overlook the nyala.

the herd bull. I suppose subconsciously, the thought of him killing three other animals influenced me.

It was the right decision. He scored out tenth in the record book; the others had been taken when there were many from which to choose. This beautiful animal stands as a full mount in my trophy room in all his beauty, proof that an animal can face extinction and still recover with careful game management.

12

Zaire-different name, same game

From the semidarkness of the thick jungle of matted vines and bushes, the figure of a huge bull bongo stood outlined in the low depression along the creek bank. The big, barefooted black man stood crouched low on the ground, pointing at the beast with a finger that shook out of sheer excitement.

He didn't say a word, just pointed. I quickly raised the .458 Browning and sent a .510 solid grain bullet into the bull's shoulder.

He bolted forward to my right, running in a crouch with his magnificent spiraled horns lying flat on his neck and his nose raised in the air. I sent another solid through the screen of leaves and bushes and heard the thud of the bullet strike home. But he still did not go down. I ran forward with a pounding heart, forcing my way through the thick bush toward a small clear spot to my right. He stood facing me with lowered head. I again shot him, this time in the chest. The great horns lowered even more as he came for me in a savage lunge.

This safari was another exclusive hunt for that most elusive of all African big game, the bongo.

I was hunting in an area that had more thick jungle than any other portion of Africa. This country is Zaire, or the ex-Belgian Congo.

Opening pages: Our hunting camp in Zaire was located in dense jungle, with trees towering high above the tents.
Opposite page: A group of young girls find great amusement in their first experience with a pair of binoculars.

211

My arrival in Kinshasa (which was formerly Leopoldville) was the fulfillment of all the dreams I had as a boy of hunting the dark and mysterious continent of Africa.

It is unfortunate that the name was changed from the Congo. No other name could possibly describe this vast jungle of thick forest — long vines hanging from tall, giant hardwood trees and the eternal dampness that always surrounds you in a humid forest that reeks with the smell of decaying wood.

However, this is the home of the western bongo, and my quest for another one of these elusive animals had led me here.

The bongo is, without a doubt, the top trophy in Africa. Many have hunted him without success. I had spent fifty-three days hunting them in the Abaderes, Mount Kenya and the Mau Range before successfully taking one. It was in the Mau Range of Njoro Kenya, accompanied by Tony Seth-Smith in 1968, that I finally took my trophy. Three years later I accidentally shot a small bongo in Liberia while hunting for royal antelope.

So before starting this hunt for bongo, I had spent some 63 days in the thick jungle of bamboo, stinging needles, biting ants and lush vegetation.

We stayed in Kinshasa for a day, then departed for Isiro, a small town northeast of Kinshasa, about 100 miles from the Sudan border.

Here we were met by Marcel Van de Bulke, the uncle of the owner of Zaire Outfitters, and our two professional white hunters, Derek MacLeod and Andre Johni. My P.W.H. for this hunt was Derek MacLeod, a young Briton who was raised in South Africa and now resided in Zambia. We shook hands at the airport, the only five white faces in a sea of blacks, and immediately proceeded to a beautiful old mansion that sat in the center of a huge coffee plantation.

The house, like so many other beautiful homes scattered throughout the country, was once the pride and joy of the Belgians who carved huge coffee plantations out of the unsettled jungle. They were forced to leave during the civil unrest and revolution that tore the country apart during the early sixties. Now all these beautiful homes are rotting and will soon be devoured by the creeping jungle that must be constantly beaten back if a clearing or building is to survive.

A flower garden choked with weeds and a rusted water fountain in the center of the curved structure were mute evidence that someone once loved this place and enjoyed the beauty and comfort it offered from the jungle surrounding it.

Next morning we were off to the hunting area, 400 kilometers northeast of Isiro. The small village is called Paika and is located near Garamba National Park.

It was a long, hot, bone-jarring ride over roads that had not been maintained since the Belgians left in 1964. When passing deep holes, we used low gear to ease the strain on the car. The ruts made the road almost impossible to travel upon.

The landscape was dotted with small mud huts with thatched roofs. Yet there were not as many structures as seen along the road in East Africa. We crossed over two large rivers on the trip. The second river, the Kibaldi, located near the nearly deserted town bearing the same name, was the scene of one of the most brutal crimes committed in the Congo during the rebellion. Two priests were beheaded and 15 nuns were beaten, raped and thrown over the bridge onto the rocks below. Several graves on a lower bank of the river remain as reminders of the tragedy. Miraculously, two of the nuns survived and later returned to the Congo to resume their work.

We ate lunch on the porch of one of the few buildings that were occupied in the town. Nearby, stood the only castle found in the Congo. It was built by three young Belgians, complete with turret, battlement walls and a

The Zaire countryside was dotted with small thatched huts.

moat. The moat, which had been dry for many years, circled the entire structure.

The town, built of beautiful red brick, must have been very magnificent in days past with its many red clay shingled roofs gleaming in the bright African sun. Derek told me it possessed all the pomp, ceremony and color that money could provide. Now deserted, all white people had gone except for two or three traders who kept stores open for the natives. No doubt, in time the jungle will reclaim all the land again, and the town will disappear.

Along the way we bought some mangos from the natives and ate them. It is one of my favorite fruits of Africa, but one must be careful not to eat too much because the acid content is high and will make your mouth sore.

We arrived at our camp near nightfall and went to bed early, tired but excited by the thought of going hunting next morning.

I was awakened by the crash of thunder and the sound of rain falling on the roof on my tent. I listened to the sound for awhile, realizing that the rain had stopped all jungle noise. But the sound of the falling rain and the knowledge that the moisture would make for good tracking quickly lulled me back to sleep.

My hunting partner on the trip was Dante Marroco. An avid hunter, he lives on the Palos Verdes Peninsula near Los Angeles. When I mentioned that I was going to the Congo and Zambia, he spoke of a great desire to hunt the same area. So I invited him to join me. He also brought along his 15-year-old son, Bob.

Our hunting camp was located in dense jungle. Tall trees towered above us and huge vines, almost a foot thick and over a hundred feet long, draped from the trees. There was a thatched shelter where we ate; the tents had been set up in small clearings. Dante and Bob's tent was new and watertight, but mine had seen too many years of service. Neither end would close and the roof leaked a bit. Yet it was still a very comfortable bongo camp.

The natives were friendly and anxious to please us. They were quite different from the people who, a few years ago had slaughtered thousands of their own tribe, raped missionary nuns and beheaded priests in a wild frenzy that lasted several years and cost more than a million lives. Many were afflicted with leprosy and had lost their toes and fingers until there were only stumps hanging from their bodies.

I also saw several natives who had elephantiasis; their legs were enormous, their scrotums swollen as large as their heads. Both diseases are

One of the Zaire inhabitants, the chimpanzee, was always anxious to make friends.

common in the Congo.

There is a large fruit bat which lives in the jungle that gives out a continuous call during the night resembling a small bongo. The call is repeated at a rapid pace like the beat of a large alarm clock. It was very difficult to get any sleep unless you could adjust to this annoying sound.

Then, between three and four o'clock in the morning, the colobus monkeys would announce their visit to the camp by loud calls. The great cats and hyenas could not be heard, but the other sounds common to the jungle more than made up for the loss.

The sound of the colobus monkeys' arrival in the trees above my tent awakened me that night. I lay listening to the sounds made by the jungle inhabitants until early dawn.

I then arose, getting my feet wet in the puddles on the floor where the water had blown in during the night. I dressed, washed up and went down the slight incline to the mess tent.

I was joined by Dante and Bob a short time later for breakfast with our professional hunters. Then we piled into the two vehicles with our boys and went looking for bongo.

Our hunting was conducted on the following schedule. Each morning the local natives were paid to go into the jungle and look for fresh spoor. Derek and I took his Land Rover while Dante and his P.W.H., Andre used a Toyota to cruise along the 15-mile stretch of road.

When a team consisting of two men found fresh spoor, they came out to the road and waited for one of the vehicles. Then the local tracker, the P.W.H. and the hunter would go and check the spoor.

I was only interested in following the tracks of a big lone bull. Derek instructed our tracker, Bitey, to inform the men of our target game.

The rain that had fallen during the night assured us that any tracks would be fresh.

We made one run along the narrow road that the Belgians had cleared through the thick bush. Natives milled around the thatched circular huts they had built along the road. The sky was a bright blue. Only a few scattered clouds could be seen. The sun rays were already starting to warm the dense jungle that would soon resemble a steam room where inhabitants constantly remained wet from their own perspiration.

After three miles of driving, we stopped and waited several minutes, then started slowly driving back down the road. We had gone only a short distance when we saw two of our boys standing on the roadside with big grins on their faces.

We stopped while Derek and our tracker, Bitey, held a brief consultation with them. "They have found the tracks of two bongo," Derek informed me. I could hardly believe it. In Kenya we would go for two or three days without striking a fresh bongo track.

Derek gave the men two packs of cigarettes apiece, the price agreed upon for finding fresh bongo spoor. I took my .458 from the boy that had been holding it in the back of the truck, slipped a bullet "up the spout" as the professionals say, and announced I was ready. It is best to be prepared the moment you enter the jungle because you can never tell when a snap shot in the thick bush may be necessary.

We went about a half mile from the road in single file, one of the boys leading, I with my rifle, then Derek, Bitey and the other boy bringing up the rear. We went through grass that grew eight feet high in open glades. Most of the light was shut out by tall trees towering above and thick vegetation growing below.

The man went straight to the spoor. A double row of heart-shaped tracks were clearly etched in the mud. There was a brief whispered consultation. Then Derek said, "A bull and a cow about two hours old."

"I will take either one," I replied. "I want a full mount of each."

Derek nodded, then held another short conference with Bitey. The tracker started out on the trail of the spoor with me only a step behind. Derek and the other two men waited at the spot where we had found the tracks. From now on, it was just a matter for the two of us, Bitey and I, pitting our skill of stalking against the alertness of the most elusive animal in the world.

Bitey moved without a sound. His eyes constantly sought spots where his bare feet could settle without breaking a limb or stirring a leaf. His eyes were constantly flickering between the ground and into the bush ahead for the slightest movement or a minute difference of color. He was seeking a small patch of chestnut red in the green and tan foliage.

I called upon all my skill of forty years of hunting and the instinct of my Indian ancestors in order to follow him as silently as possible.

We did a good job. We came upon the two bongo after a couple hours of steady tracking. The wet patches of the rain had vanished due to the hot rays of the tropical sun and a gentle breeze that constantly changed directions.

Bitey would frequently stop to listen. I watched him in admiration as the big wooly head turned from side to side, canting slightly forward as he listened. In my mind I thought here is the real hunter of man's world. He moves more quietly than an animal, sees as well and hears almost as well. And while he cannot smell his prey, his eyes are so good that no game can elude him unless the animal travels over solid rock for a long distance. Truly this man and others like him are the greats of the Weatherby Award and other hunting trophies.

Bitey heard something. We stood frozen for a moment. He was in the process of raising his hand when the wind blowing from our right slightly changed direction. I now felt it on the back of my neck. There was an

instant explosion of movement in front of us, not more that 25 feet away. With a grunt and the pounding of hooves, the bongo were gone.

Bitey turned with a smile on his face, his white teeth bright against the blackness of his face. He shook his head, indicating by a wave of his hand that the wind had given us away. We started back trailing the way we had come. In fifteen minutes we met Derek and the others.

I explained to Derek what had happened as we headed for the truck. My sense of direction had deserted me. The bongo had meandered about nibbling at fresh leaves on vines and plants, changing directions many times. The boys hit the road not more than a half mile from the Land Rover.

The next day Derek awoke with an attack of malaria. But like the determined Scot he is, he insisted that we go hunting. We found fresh tracks again quite early, but this time I took the three boys with me while Derek stayed in the Land Rover. He was much too sick to walk.

The boys had found the track of a lone bongo. I couldn't tell if it was a

The men and boys of the village, including their pet dog, carry their nets in anticipation of carrying back some small game.

cow or a young bull, but we followed it for two hours until it led us to a set of fifteen bongo spoor. We followed them and found where the animals had rested but had then moved on again.

Bitey put his hand on the ground where one had been lying to feel for warmth. He lifted his hand in the air, waving it away from us while shaking his head.

It was plain to see what he was trying to say. Either the breeze had given us away or one of the bongos had seen or heard us and scattered the herd. They had slipped away quietly and there was no possibility of trailing them.

On the way back we came upon another lone track. We followed it for about three hours before giving it up. Bitey simply explained the decision by stopping suddenly, then waving his hand outward.

I have hunted enough to know that he was attempting to say the animal was "a traveler," he had his mind set on a distant place he wanted to go to. We would never be able to locate him. When we returned to the Land Rover, Derek was very sick. I drove the vehicle back to camp as quickly as possible.

That night it rained again and my tent leaked badly. Water literally washed through the tent. I had to get up and move some of my gear along with my bed to keep them dry.

Daylight dawned sharp and clear. Derek could not get out of bed. He was very ill. Not only was he suffering from malaria, but he also had severe stomach cramps. The Congo has always been hard on the white man. I had lumps on the back of my neck where ants had dropped down from the trees and stung me. The bites I had scratched from flies and mosquitos were beginning to fester, and I had only been in the country five days.

The boys and I went hunting while Derek remained in camp. Again fresh bongo tracks were spotted near the end of the road we had hunted the day before. We followed them. It was a full herd this time, and although we came up on them as carefully as possible, they again bolted before I could see well enough to shoot.

We returned to the Land Rover at about twelve o'clock and started back to camp. We were almost there when two of our trackers stopped us.

Bitey was not too impressed, but the boys were persistent. We finally left the Land Rover and followed them through the tall grass into the jungle. It was a lone bull and the tracks were gigantic, much larger than any I had ever seen. I could tell even Bitey was now impressed.

They were very fresh, too. Here was an old bull wandering around in the middle of the day. Bitey and I went forward while the other two stayed well behind.

We came to a natural salt lick in the dense jungle where the bull had stopped to lick the ground. He had then proceeded into a small stream that ran silently through the thick tangle of bush and vines. A bunch of bright yellow butterflies rose in a cloud of fluttering wings from the moist salt ground as we walked by.

The huge, heart-shaped tracks of the bull led into the water. I am sure the cool stream felt good on Bitey's bare feet. After the first steps into the water, my tennis shoes were filled, but I didn't mind at all.

Bitey silently pointed upward to show where the bull had taken a bite off of an overhanging branch. He constantly kept a sharp watch on each bank to see where the bull had left the water. Then we both saw it at the same time. There was a track about six inches deep near the edge of the stream where he had climbed up the bank.

Small drops of water were still seeping through the mud and sliding down into the bull track. Bitey and I exchanged looks. He made the age-old gesture to go quietly by moving both hands slowly up and down.

I pulled my .458 forward, leaving my right thumb on safety as we eased up the bank over the slight ridge into the low depression along the creek bed. It was there that Bitey dropped to the ground in front of me and pointed. We had found the bull.

As I ran after the bongo, I completely forgot any danger from such a large bull. I managed to get off three shots before he turned to charge. I was totally unprepared for his attack. Even if I had been, I would not have had time to get the fourth and final bullet into the chamber. Only 20 to 25 feet separated me from the charging animal. I automatically stepped aside in that last split second before he would have hit me.

He plunged into the mass of tangled vines and bush behind me and fell to his knees, mortally wounded by the three .458 solids in his body. When he struggled to his feet, I quickly slipped my last shell from the magazine into the spout. As the bull turned toward me, I shot him in the neck. He fell about three feet away from me.

Bitey came running into the small clearing and grabbed me in his arms. He hugged and lifted me off the ground in his excitement. He had seen the bull's charge and the climax of the action.

A short time later the other two men arrived. After looking at the size of the bull, both became excited and embraced me. Then one of them disappeared into the bush. Within an hour we had lots of visitors, including Dante, Bobby, Johnny and even Derek, who had gotten out of his sickbed to see the bongo. I was very surprised to learn that we were only three miles from our camp.

We measured the bull's horns. They made the record book with a length of 29-3/8 inches. The base of the horns were huge, measuring over 13 inches in girth, the largest on record. The top of the horns, which are usually flared, had almost been flattened by the constant rubbing he had given them butting anthills. He was a very old bull. I would guess his weight at about 800 pounds. Derek and I measured him. He stood 53 inches at the shoulder and was 81 inches long from his horns to his tail. His neck measured 54 inches in girth at the shoulder and his belly measured 81 inches in circumference. He was a magnificent animal, indeed.

Derek and I stayed at the Paika camp one more day before we decided to

Finally we capture the long awaited trophy which had evaded us in so many previous hunts — the bongo.

leave the area. We left all the help with Dante so he would have a good chance of scoring. We went back to headquarters in Isiro and hunted out of the farmhouse, getting up at 3 A.M. in the morning and driving 50 to 60 miles each day in order to hunt.

On one occasion during a rainstorm, Derek and his man became separated from me and my two aides. It wasn't long before we were completely lost in the downpour. It's an interesting experience to get lost in the Belgian Congo's vast jungle, especially during a major rainstorm. It took over three hours for us to find our way back to the trail.

On the third day of the hunt, a small young black who was serving as my tracker came upon a lone female bongo. Although I could only see a small patch of red in the thick bush, I decided to fire a bullet into it.

I was amazed to see my young friend go up a tree like a squirrel when the bongo began to thrash about in the brush near us. Then I remembered the savage rush of the bull at me only a few days earlier and I understood and sympathized with him. After all, he was unarmed while I carried a loaded rifle in my hands.

Derek had also told me that the natives considered the bongo a vicious and aggressive animal. Some people were killed each year by them.

It again took four shots to kill the bongo. I never had a clear shot until the fourth bullet. I had followed the blood spoor several hundred yards before I found the bongo almost at the point of death.

She was a beautiful animal with slender spiral horns, much prettier than the bull because of her red and white striped skin.

Yet, there was not the thrill in taking this bongo as there had been with the big bull. But the opportunity of taking two bongo during one trip is always an exciting occasion, and it is a great conclusion to a very successful hunt.

The female bongo was much more beautiful than the male because of her long, spiral horns and bright red and white striped skin.

Too late for trophies in Zambia

Zambia is a country I hunted after its prime, I am sure. And I am not sure that I hunted the best area when I did hunt it. If I did, it does not compare with several other African countries I have hunted such as Kenya and Tanganyika, and certainly not with Angola.

When I decided to hunt Zambia, I selected the Laungwa Valley as a specific location. I had taken all of the animals native to Zambia except a plain, ordinary antelope called the puku, found only in Zambia, predominantly in the Laungwa Valley.

I arrived in Lusaka along with one of my hunting friends, Dante Marrocco, and his son Bob. We had just completed a bongo hunt in Zaire. We were met by the Laungwa Valley Safaris representative and taken to the Intercontinental Hotel.

The next morning we were flown down to a small village where our professional hunters awaited us. A young man just starting his career, Adrian Carr, and an old-timer well known to the hunting world, Angelo Dacey, who was born in the Sudan, were our two guides.

As we had lunch, I could see that the company had arranged for me to hunt with Angelo and Dante would have the younger man. As I had shot

Opening pages: Wildebeest graze quietly on the open plain.
Opposite page: A lioness stalks the tall brush for game.

two bongo in Zaire and Dante had not been so lucky, I was determined that he would have the best possible chance on this safari. So I engaged young Adrian in conversation and when we left the small eating place, I climbed into the Land Rover with him.

As we drove along I questioned him about his father, Norman Carr, who is a well known figure in Africa. We had a pleasant chat and he finally said, "Mr. McElroy, I am supposed to guide Mr. Marrocco."

"I know that," I answered. "However, unless you object, you and I will hunt together."

"I would be very glad to hunt with you, but Mr. Smith is the boss," he answered.

"I will speak to him," I said.

On the way to the main hunting camp and commissary, the road passes through a large game preserve that follows the Laungwa River. Game was very plentiful. I saw good herds of puku, buffalo, waterbuck, impala and a few kudu. Small herds of elephant were everywhere.

I have never seen so many hippo. Several crocodile occupied each sandbar that projected out into the valley. I was thrilled to see so much game and looked forward to starting the hunt. The great hunting to be had in Zambia seemed, at last, to be a reality.

Adrian stopped at a spot along the road. We walked about 50 yards into the grass and looked at a small headstone stuck into the ground. It read "Arnold White killed by an elephant 1929." The marker was mute evidence that often the hunter becomes the victim of the hunted.

We crossed the Laungwa River twice before coming to the main camp of Laungwa Safaris. There I was introduced to Frank Smith, director of Laungwa Safaris, his wife and another young couple, who were the managers of the three camps of Laungwa Safaris and the commissary of supplies.

While we were having a drink under a small arbor adjacent to the main building, a tsetse fly settled on Bob and bit him. He slapped at the fly and the director smiled.

"You will find we have quite a lot of those in certain areas," he said.

"They really bite," Bob said, rubbing his arm.

"We don't have many in the camps," Smith said. "We cleared out the bush nearby and they don't often come in where there is no cover."

I asked Smith if Adrian and I could hunt together. He said that was up to me. I am quite sure I offended Angelo, but I was really paying him a compliment. I knew he was by far the most experienced professional hunter, but I wanted Dante to have the benefit of his great experience.

We left the main camp soon after we finished our drink and again followed the river until we arrived at a pontoon ferry. It was constructed of empty oil barrels and anchored to a cable stretched across the river.

We drove the Land Rover on the barge and crossed by pulling the barge along the cable by hand. It moved easily because the river current was very slow. In a few minutes we arrived in camp, located on the river overlooking a sandbar, just out of sight of the crossing.

The location was the usual permanent camp in Zambia and Botswana. A small cluster of grass and reed huts were set in a circle. A thick woven grass fence about six feet high had been built on the bush side of the camp. I never did understand why it was there except perhaps to deter wandering prides of lion or a herd of elephant following the river.

It certainly wouldn't have kept them out because the entrance was kept open, and the fence stopped short of the sandy beach on each side.

We were introduced to Angelo's wife, a small woman who seldom had much to say, but always accompanied Angelo whenever he hunted. They had some children who were not very old in Kaurtoum, but they stayed with their grandmother. We also met the camp staff of six boys, the cook, helper and other camp help. After a very nice dinner we turned in. I dropped off to sleep with the lonely wail of a hungry hyena drifting through my mind.

Next morning Adrian and I pulled out of camp before sunrise and drove upstream about three miles from camp. We had decided to shoot a hippo for lion bait and leave it while we hunted other game. He was very surprised when I told him my prime reason for coming to Zambia was to take a good puku. He pointed out that under the game laws of Zambia I must pay about $1,100 for all species including lion, leopard and elephant, even if I did not take them. This, of course, is a bad law. It encourages taking animals that one is not interested in. Ethiopia has the best license law. You must pay for a general license, then pay an additional sum for the game you have shot.

I reluctantly agreed to shoot some lion bait. The hippo was a good choice because there were too many in the valley. The game department was planning to harvest some 2,000 of them in the near future.

We arrived at a spot by the river where we left the Land Rover. Accompanied by two boys we walked along the bank to a shallow wash. It was filled with grass. The brush had grown tall around the potholes of stagnant water that were slowly drying up. On either side of the wash the thick bush and trees grew high. The grunting sounds of feeding hippo came from the banks of both sides of the wash. They had come out of the river to eat the grass but would return by early in the morning to remain all day.

Adrian was leading the way as we walked in single file through the trees. The sounds of the early morning birds, such as the fish eagle, were occasionally broken by the raucous cry of a baboon.

Suddenly, without any warning, there was a fierce growl. We stopped in our tracks. Again it came from up in the trees. Then a leopard streaked down a slightly bent tree, reversed his direction, ran up the tree, then back down and disappeared into the bush below.

I had stepped to one side when the growl first came, but no one could have hit that black and gold flash as it raced down, up and down again like a streak. It was totally unexpected.

We had selected the area around the Laungwa Valley as our hunting site because of the game which had been spotted there.

When the leopard disappeared, Adrian also changed directions, going to the right, completely clear of the bush. We stopped, and by using our binoculars, we found his kill, a young impala wedged in the usual fork of a limb.

Without a word being spoken, we continued on to the lagoons that lay about 500 yards away.

We reached the wash and eased along the bank, keeping to the trees. Within 50 yards a huge bulk detached itself from other early morning shadows and slowly ambled toward the river. Adrian had his binoculars to his eyes.

"It's a bull," he whispered. "Shoot him."

I moved forward about ten steps so I could get a clear view and put a .458 solid into his shoulder. He stumbled, then moved faster toward the river, passing in front of me at about 40 yards. Again I hit him with a .458 solid. He stopped and spun around. Then I stepped out and shot him in the forehead. His two-ton bulk hit the ground with a thud. He didn't move again.

He had dropped under some tall trees that were clear of underbrush, about 40 yards from the tall grass and a small pond of water. On the other side some brush grew under the trees another 40 yards away, making an ideal spot to build a blind. The approach wasn't bad either. The only bad spot was about 50 yards of open area where we would have to come through some tall grass. It would not be too pleasant in the very early morning before sunup if we got a big pride of lions feeding and they scattered. However, one must take a few chances in order to approach downwind when coming to a bait.

The four of us cut tall grass and limbs from the bushes, in order to cover him up from the vultures that would soon appear in the sky looking for food. All the sounds of the hippo had ceased and the forest was quiet. We finished the blind and stood back to survey it.

"It's a good job," Adrian said, putting on a final heavy piece of wood one of the men had brought him. I agreed, then asked what he thought about the leopard growling at us. "I think he was very angry because we disturbed his breakfast," he replied.

"I have never heard one leopard make that much noise," I said. "I think there are two leopards, or the action of that leopard is very unusual."

"Perhaps," Adrian replied. "He probably won't return, however, we will have a look on the way back."

I picked up my .300 and handed my .458 to one of the men. With Adrian in the lead, we began retracking our steps toward the leopard's kill. One of the boys left small pieces of paper on limbs and grass to mark our way to the blind. We would need the markers in the semidarkness of the early morning when we came to check our lion bait.

We eased along, not really believing that the leopard would be in the tree again. However, when we were within 100 yards of the tree, he flashed down the tree and disappeared into the bush. We continued on past the tree, keeping in the clear until we were well beyond the kill.

Adrian stopped and said, "He is a very hungry and determined leopard. Do you want to try for him?"

"Yes, let's give him a try," I said. "How about the old trick of numbers?"

"Just what I had in mind," the young man smiled.

So we went back again, this time on the river side, where there was more cover. We talked continuously and made no attempt to be quiet. When we were within 50 yards of the bait tree, Adrian and I dove under a bush while the other two men continued to talk and make noise. We hoped the leopard was not watching us. Even if he was, four men going behind a thick bush and two coming out shouldn't mean much to him. After all, leopards are not supposed to count.

The sound of the two men diminished until complete silence returned to the area. I was trying to see the dead impala in the tree. However, there was a big limb in the way. Only the legs and the nose of the animal were visible behind the large branch. I could not move to improve my view. The bush was too small.

Adrian touched my knee as the head of the leopard appeared. He was standing over his kill, looking in the direction the men had taken. His tail stuck out on the other side of the limb.

Adrian looked at me in silence for an answer, but I shook my head. I could not see the leopard's body, and I certainly would not shoot him in the head and ruin the skull. So we waited while the big cat fed on the impala.

A vulture came flapping down and settled on a nearby tree. He began watching both the feeding leopard and us, cocking his head from side to side. I thought to myself, if he suddenly takes flight and the leopard comes out of the tree, I will be ready. Leopards are unpredictable.

In the distance came the sound of human voices. Three villagers, carrying fish taken from a set line and nets dangling from a pole, came into view. The tail of the leopard disappeared as he again came down the tree.

When the men were about to pass us, Adrian and I moved quickly behind another bush where I could get a clear view of the dead impala. I wondered if the leopard was determined enough to come back.

We didn't have long to wait. Within ten minutes after the men disappeared in the distance, he was back. This time his head was pointed in our direction. That's all I could see as he lay in the fork of the tree just below the bait. I felt he had either seen us move or was near enough to hear us.

We lay absolutely still. He stared down for a few moments, then raised up to expose his left shoulder. As he looked to his right, I put the cross hairs on the point of his shoulder and squeezed the trigger. At the roar of the rifle, he gave a savage growl and disappeared from sight. From below the tree came another wheezing growl or two. Then all was silent. "Where did you hit him?" Adrian whispered.

"On the left shoulder," I answered. "Let's go look at him."

"No, no," he said, "We will go back and wait."

I looked at him in wonder, knowing full well the leopard must have been killed by the 180-grain bullet that passed through his shoulder and chest. What I didn't know was that in the past four years, five clients or hunters had been mauled by a leopard in the Laungwa valley. These incidents had made all of the professionals very jittery about leopards.

Of course, he lacked experience because of his young age. He should have been watching the leopard very closely through his binoculars. He could have seen him drop out of the tree, instead of springing out as a wounded leopard would do.

Reluctantly, I followed him as he backed away toward the Land Rover. There we found the three men waiting. After a brief consultation in the local language, the men collected pangas from the Land Rover and made plans to follow Adrian to the location of the blind. I picked up my rifle and started to join them when the young hunter stopped me.

"I would consider it a favor if you would stay here," Adrian said.

"Why?" I asked.

"The leopard may not be dead; if you get mauled I may lose my license."

"But that's my leopard," I said, "and it's also my responsibility."

"Not so in Zambia," he answered. "I would very much like you to stay here."

I debated a moment, bowed my neck and came close to insisting on returning for the animal. Then I shrugged my shoulders and said, "If that's the way you prefer it. I just know the leopard is dead."

He shouldered his gun and followed the three men . . . a handsome young dedicated hunter protecting his client. Little did he know that I probably had faced more charging and dangerous animals on my many hunts in Africa and other parts of the world than he possibly could have seen in his short career as a professional hunter. Such is youth.

I sat down in the shade of a tree and waited, thinking of the few short seconds in which I centered the scope on the leopard and pulled the trigger. I was positive that I had killed this cat with one shot as I had done with eight other leopards before him. A half hour passed before Adrian walked out of the bush followed by the three men. Two of them carried a pole on which they had tied a very dead, dark leopard. He had been shot through the point of the right shoulder, and could not have lived more than a minute after hitting the ground. The growls were his last breath.

There was a moment of strained silence. I had not completely forgiven him for his actions, but then I thought, "What the hell. He was doing what he thought was best."

"He was completely dead," he said, in an apologetic tone.

"I knew he was," I answered. "He had to be, the way he dropped out of the tree."

"But we have many incidents with leopard in this area," he said. "We have to be careful."

I snapped a picture of the leopard after the boys had stretched him out on the ground. Then we climbed into the Land Rover and headed back to the camp. "Not bad for the first morning," Adrian said. He was glancing sideways at me as we rode along.

"Nope," I answered in a negative tone. "However, what I want is a record book puku."

"We will get you one," he assured me.

"You do that and I will forgive you," I answered.

Back at camp we turned the leopard over to the skinner and had some lunch in the round, grass-thatched dining room overlooking the river.

What may seem to be an exceptional photograph taken in Zambia of a leopard attacking a bushbuck is in reality a recreation of a night kill found in the McElroy Trophy Room in Tucson, Arizona.

Below us was a point of white sand that stretched about 400 yards down to the river's edge. A big crocodile lay sunning himself, his mouth wide open while a small white bird cleaned out the leaches that were stuck to his gums. I remembered Karl Luthy, an old crocodile hunter, telling me about shooting over a crocodile's head to see if he would snap his jaws on the bird cleaning his teeth. Karl assured me that the croc ran with his mouth open until the bird took wing. I suspect this was the truth because these small birds moved in and around the long sharp teeth with absolute confidence.

After lunch, Adrian and I drove a long way upriver to a big open glade that had once held water. Now it was dry and filled with short grass. We stopped the Land Rover in the bushes and moved forward to see what was in the open glade.

I quickly located some wildebeest on the other side of the glade. A small herd of impala stood motionless in the shade of a tree. "There is a herd of puku I am looking for," Adrian said, pointing off to the right.

I swung my binoculars in the direction he pointed and picked up a large herd of the small red antelope standing in the fringe of trees.

"We will wait; they will move out to graze in another hour," Adrian said.

We stood and glassed the wide open space, finding several small herds of zebra, impala, warthog and puku. On the farthest fringe of trees, a solitary bull buffalo stood motionless.

When the sun dipped below the tops of the trees an hour later, the still figures of animals began to stir. The impala moved first, coming out from their shade tree to nibble at the grass while keeping a sharp lookout for predators. The wildebeest stirred restlessly. Then, for no reason at all, they broke into a long loping gallop and ran halfway around the clearing to a sudden stop. Their movements are always unpredictable.

Two warthogs began to eat grass under the shade of a tree. The herd of puku moved leisurely out into the open, some grazing while others kept watch in the same manner as the impala. The lone bull buffalo continued to stand and stare into the clearing.

Adrian followed the herd of puku with his binoculars. "The buck that I wanted you to see is in this herd," he said.

I glassed the herd and settled on three males standing a short distance from the other animals. I saw at a glance that these were old bucks and larger than any in the herd.

"Those three together look the best," I said.

"The center one is the one I had in mind," he answered.

"I agree that he is the best, but will he make the book? Remember, we need 17 inches."

"I know of only one other who may be better," he answered. "The only way to tell is to shoot him."

We moved forward, keeping to the edge of the trees, but the puku fed into the center of the open space before we were within shooting range. We lined up the bucks with a large tree that grew in the open and approached slowly, keeping the tree between us. Our approach would not have worked with most game, but the puku is a somewhat stupid animal and does not spook easily.

We got to within 200 yards of the three animals and studied them again. Not being familiar with the puku, I was at a loss at guessing the length of their horns. By comparing them to an impala, they look pretty short.

"What do you think?" I asked.

"If the dark red one won't make it, it will surprise me," he answered.

I raised my rifle, shot him and walked out to where he had dropped. I pulled my tape measure out of my pocket and laid it on the ridged horns. It read 16¼ inches.

"Looks like we are a little short," I said.

"I thought he would make it," Adrian said. "I am sorry."

"We have another chance," I said. "We will have plenty of time to look them over."

The boys had begun the slow process of driving the Land Rover across the open glade. The deep tracks made by elephant and other heavy animals during the wet season, had turned the open area into an obstacle course. We sat down and waited about ten minutes before they reached us. When the Land Rover arrived at the spot where the puku dropped, the boys started to clean him out, while Adrian and I glassed the far side of the dried marsh. We both found the heavy black line of animals advancing from the forest at the same time. It was a herd of buffalo that numbered several hundred.

"Let's go look at them," Adrian suggested. We left the Land Rover partly hidden by a fallen tree and walked toward the buffalo, keeping in line with the fallen tree.

We came within 300 yards of the huge mass of powerful bodies and stopped just behind the fallen tree. The wind was blowing in our direction, bringing with it the low sounds made by the cows to the calves. The herd continued to feed parallel to us. It was an ideal setup; the herd was careless and hungry after lying in the thickets all day.

They fed along, led by an old cow and flanked by old bulls. Several of them brought up the rear. All heads were never down at the same time. The old lead cow seldom fed as she moved slowly forward with her nose in the air and black eyes looking at the shadows along the tree line.

There were several good bulls in the herd, but not within shooting distance. How could we find a way of getting any closer? I wasn't too keen on taking a buffalo unless he possessed an unusually good head. I had shot several book animals and one that went over 50 inches in spread and 48 inches in length.

"Have you had enough?" Adrian asked.

"Yes, they are always magnificent," I answered.

We both stepped around the fallen tree and the herd instantly froze. Then several of the bulls turned to face us, their black noses lifted in the air sniffing at the breeze, their fierce eyes fixed on us. Adrian waved his arm and the entire black mass of buffalo exploded. They raced for the trees raising a huge cloud of dust that partly hid the beautiful red glare on the

Zambia also yielded this fine roan with a good set of horns.

horizon where the sun had just set. It was a magnificent sight and one that I never tire of remembering.

We were up very early next morning, earlier than usual because the big cats are known to leave a bait soon after daylight. The Land Rover moved along noiselessly through the semidarkness of early morning along the river as we headed in the direction of our lion bait. Overhead, a flock of birds swept by with raucous cries on their way to a small lagoon further downstream. The grunts of feeding hippo came from the tall grass in a bend of the river.

Early morning in any country is always the best time of the day, but in Africa with its many forest sounds, from the roar of a lion to the chirp of its many birds, it is absolutely superb.

We stopped. Without a sound, Adrian, I and two boys got out. With one leading and the other in the rear of the line, we silently moved through the trees into a shallow ditch and the tall grass of the lagoon. The small bits of white paper served as beacons in the sea of grass.

We emerged from the brush and were back into the fringe of woods. The tall Negro dropped back and Adrian took the lead. I was directly behind him, proceeding cautiously one step at a time guided by the small bits of paper.

Suddenly Adrian and I were alone as the two other men dropped off under a big tree in silence. We again came to a small stretch of tall grass. Crossing it, we reached the second group of trees and our small blind where the dead hippo lay. The air blew gently on my face; it was a good setup and the wind was right.

We came up behind the small wall of leaves and brush the boys had constructed. Adrian peeked through the hole into the shadows beneath the trees in front of us. He shook his head and stepped back as I looked through it. I could see nothing in the darkness of the tree shadows. Then the sound of a bone being cracked by powerful jaws and a low guttural growl were heard.

We stood motionless, waiting to see what was going on out in front of us. It was 60 yards away; I remembered I stepped it off before leaving the place the previous morning. The young professional had made a mistake and brought us to the blind too early. He had forgotten that the dead hippo lay under tall trees that blotted out the early morning light. Now there were lions in front of us and could be any place near, but we could not see them. A feeding lion, especially a female with cubs, is not an animal to take liberties with or you may regret it.

The light increased slowly as the sun began to rise in the east. Finally we were able to see the dead hippo which had been uncovered. A beautiful huge lioness with three half-grown cubs were busy tearing a huge hole in the belly of the hippo. A few feet away a second female with four smaller cubs lay waiting for their turn. I was happy that we had not stumbled into one of these families in the darkness, especially the lioness with the little cubs.

We watched silently as the animals satisfied their hunger. The big lioness suddenly stopped feeding, gathered her three cubs and walked away toward the lagoon to drink. The other lioness took over her spot while the four little cubs gamboled about, wrestling and chasing each other.

I wondered how long it would be before one chased the other into our blind and what the results would be.

Adrian must have been thinking the same thing for he began backing away slowly. I was only too happy to follow. We returned the way we had come and soon reached the other two men we had left behind. Adrian and the men held a short conversation and then said, "One of the men saw these two females last week and there is a good male with them."

"I didn't see him," I answered.

"He may be lying in the tall grass near the lagoon," he answered. "You know the male always eats first and he may have gone for a drink. We will wait for awhile and go back for a look."

So we sat down and waited about half an hour. The sun was just peeking over the horizon and all the night shadows had disappeared. Adrian got up, grabbed his rifle and started back following the paper trail. I followed him after checking my rifle again to make sure I had a bullet up the spout even though I knew there was one in there.

We again came to the blind without incident. Both of us peeked through the hole together. There was not a lion in sight. We looked at each other and Adrian straightened up while I looked back at the dead hippo. Then something resembling a whip with a fringe of hair on the end raised up from the far side of the hippo. It was obvious that a lone lion was feeding on the carcass.

I motioned for Adrian to look again. We both watched for about five minutes. The tail would raise up in the air each time the lion pulled off a bite of meat. It was almost funny observing a tail of an animal that we couldn't see. As we continued following his actions, he suddenly stood up. I could see he had a fair mane, at least better than the usual wild African lion.

Adrian looked questionably at me. I put my mouth close to his ear and whispered, "Do you think we can do better?"

He shook his head, "Not likely in this area."

"I will take him then," I answered. It was as though he had heard me for the lion moved from where he had been eating to where the females had been. His body was now square with me, but his head turned a bit to the right on an angle. I put the cross hairs just behind his left shoulder and pulled the trigger.

At the crash of the rifle, he let out a tremendous roar. His hind legs propelled him straight up into the air, at least five feet clear off the ground and over the dead hippo. He then ran almost in a circle (the usual action of a heart shot) and headed back to our blind, stopping in some bush a few yards to our left.

Adrian and I had quickly backed away from the blind as I jacked another bullet into the chamber. We stood in the open, a few steps from the blind and about thirty steps away from where the lion disappeared. The sound of his labored breathing was very clear and loud. We waited another few minutes and the sound died away. We then approached carefully after Adrian had thrown two sticks into the small bush where he lay.

He was dead. The bullet had entered just where it should have — at that angle just behind the front leg, through the heart and out on the point of the right front shoulder. "A good shot," Adrian commented.

The boys arrived and within minutes were busy removing his skin. Adrian and I went down to the river where a big herd of hippo were crowded together in one small area.

We stopped on the bank overlooking the animals and Adrian remarked, "It's strange how they like to live in a certain small section of the river. We call them 'hippo pools'."

"I know," I answered. "But how about that one over on the sandbar?"

"He has been kicked out of the herd by the herd bull, " he answered.

"I wonder why?"

"Who knows, perhaps he challenged the head man or tried to cut in on his harem."

"Looks like the outcast is coming in," I said.

"He is," Adrian said. "Now you will see him chased."

The lone bull came toward the other hippo. Down below another huge bull left the center of the group and moved forward to meet him. The outcast moved across the sandbar and into the shallow water about 35 yards from the herd. He seemed determined to join them.

The herd bull reached the shallow end of the pool and emerged from the depths to stand in knee deep water facing the other hippo who had stopped. For a moment they remained facing each other. Then the herd bull lunged forward through the shallow water with his tremendous mouth wide open. For a moment the lone bull stood his ground, then turned and fled with the herd bull in full chase.

They moved through the water and up on the sandbar like two locomotives, making the sand fly with their huge feet. Then the lone bull turned a circle near the far bank with the herd bull in hot pursuit. He came racing back and plunged into the water among the other hippos. The herd bull was right on his tail. Huge bodies were whirling in and out among the other hippos who were knocked about like tenpins. I looked at Adrian who was obviously enjoying this titanic battle.

The herd was scattered by the battle. A few hippos left the pool to stand on the sandbar out of range of the two combatants. The battle stopped as suddenly as it had begun, as the outcast shot out of the water and ran up the sandbar a hundred feet from the herd. The herd bull quit chasing the

Not too many gals would turn their back on the king of the jungle, but this one did!

intruder the moment he left the water.

Young Adrian smiled at me. "Some battle, right?"

"A lot of weight was thrown around," I agreed.

"Sometimes they kill each other," he said, as we shouldered our guns and started back for the dead lion.

On the way to camp Adrian pulled off the trail and went down to the river. He stopped in the fringe of trees that hid a lone stretch of open grass. It ended in a long sandbar that projected out into the river.

"This is where the other big puku lives," he said, getting out of the car.

"I hope he is at least an inch better than our first," I answered.

"If he won't make it, I don't know of another that will," Adrian stated.

"We have eighteen more days," I said. "We can look over every puku in this valley."

"We will have to before we shoot this one," he said.

They were there, about 150 beautiful reddish tan animals, almost too stupid to run until too late. I really don't know how they survive the lion prides and leopards in the valley. Adrian said they seldom ventured into the woods and kept sentries posted for the big cats. I suppose that was true or they wouldn't last long.

We found him right away. He was a proud buck, quite dark with a good set of deeply ridged horns that curved back and out at the tips. "What do you think?" Adrian asked after I had put the glasses on him.

"I wouldn't bet on it," I said. "However, I believe he is better than the first."

"I do too, but let's look for a few days. I want to see if we can find some more big ones. I have had clients that wanted big leopard, big elephant and lion, but never one who wanted a big puku before."

We returned to the Land Rover and drove back to camp where we met Dante and Bob who had returned to camp for a hot meal.

Dante's first words to me were, "You lucky stiff, a leopard the first day and a lion the next."

"Be patient, Dante, your turn will come," I said. "I would almost guarantee you will have a good hunt."

The prediction came true for within the next ten days he collected lion, elephant and a buffalo. He also took a leopard that gave us all a little excitement for awhile.

He and Angelo had a leopard feeding in a large tree which grew on the bank of a sandy wash. Across the wash was a flat open area that was covered with tall grass and thick bush. The cat came to the bait very late. Dante couldn't see him too well but decided to shoot as the cat was standing on a limb facing him. He shot and the cat disappeared. After waiting a few minutes, he and Angelo approached the tree and found a spot of blood where the cat had fallen out of the tree. It had already become dark so they decided the only sensible thing to do was return to the camp.

Adrian and I accompanied them to the spot the next morning to help search for the cat. A wounded leopard is not a pleasant plaything and is probably the most dangerous of any wild animal when wounded. The spot of blood was under the tree. We began to cautiously circle around to find a blood spoor. It was Angelo who found a small blood smear on the sand where the cat had climbed the bank. We now knew he had gone into the grass and bush on the flat area. We held a short council of war.

I had a .458 with a detachable scope which I had removed and now had open sights as did the two professional hunters. Dante only carried his .300 with a scope which was almost useless at close range of 10 to 15 feet which was the range we expected the cat to come at us. So it was decided that the three of us — Adrian, Angelo and myself — would go in a line about four or five feet apart. Dante would follow close behind us and shoot only if we saw the cat some distance away. I personally consider it almost criminal for a camp to not have a shotgun for just such emergencies. It's great insurance and about the only sensible way to hunt a wounded leopard. We moved forward, pausing to look closely at each small bunch of grass and each small bush. It was a slow, tedious march under pressure. I tried to remain as loose as I could and still hold the heavy rifle at the ready.

Proceeding side by side, it took us at least 30 minutes to cover the first 50 yards. Then another 30 minutes elapsed while we backtracked over another 14 feet. We saw nothing. It was time to go into the thicker grass and bush where we could see only a few yards in front of us.

Angelo, being the oldest professional, made the decision: "We are not going into that thick stuff," he said. "Let's bring up a motorcar."

Adrian went back and returned in his Land Rover. Angelo and his gun bearer climbed up on the roof. Adrian drove, Dante sat in the center and I took the outside as we went back looking for the cat.

We made two trips, driving up and down the small area of grass and bush at a slow pace.

I was straining my eyes, peering under each possible hiding place a leopard could crouch. Suddenly there was an explosion just over my head and a leopard rolled practically under the tip of my rifle. He had blended so well with the dead yellow grass that I looked over the top of him. So did Angelo until his gun bearer saw the leopard.

We left the Land Rover and gathered about the cat to examine where he had been hit. Adrian voiced the question I was thinking. "Why didn't the leopard come for us as they usually do?" That was clearly explained as soon as I looked at the dead cat.

Dante's bullet had missed the chest of the leopard. It had gone upward and entered the flank between the hind leg and the belly and came up through the muscle about 18 inches from the tip.

The wound would not have been fatal and would have probably healed in a short time. However, the tail had been broken which took all the fight out of the leopard. It is the most sensitive part of a cat. If Dante had not broken the tail and we had come onto him lying in the grass, he would have been in our laps in one leap.

I have observed other cats with broken tails; they lose all the spirit to fight or hunt until the tail heals. We were lucky this time.

My hunt was for twenty-one days. I spent eighteen of those days looking at puku up and down the river. We saw a good two or three thousand of them. Adrian and I also looked at many elephant and buffalo, but I didn't shoot any as I did not find a good trophy in the herds I saw. However, we did have an interesting experience with a crocodile.

I had told Adrian that I wanted to shoot a crocodile among the hundreds along the river. Some were gigantic in size. On two or three occasions, we stalked the reptiles as they lay on the sandbars, only to have them slip into the water before we were within shooting range. Then one afternoon we saw two beyond a point that offered cover within about 150 yards. They were on the other side of the river, as was their normal pattern of behavior. We glassed them before we made the stalk.

"One of them is very big," Adrian said. "About three feet longer than the other one." We crawled on our stomachs up to the last bunch of grass overlooking the point. Adrian rose slightly and took a look. "The one nearest us is the bigger one," he whispered. I eased the .300 up until I could see the sandbar, moving until the cross hairs in the scope were just under the knob containing the crocodile's brains and squeezed off.

After the sound of the explosion, I raised my head in order to see the sandbar. One crocodile's tail was waving feebly while the other was sliding into the water.

Adrian's voice was reproachful in my ear. "You shot the wrong croc; the other was much larger."

I thought this was funny and laughed before answering. "One croc's head looks very much like another through a scope, Adrian."

"But the other's head was much larger," he persisted.

"They were laying side by side and one pretty well blended into the other," I answered. "How are we going to get that one now?"

"I don't believe I can get the boys to go into the river with that big one still alive and near," he answered.

"Don't do it if it's dangerous," I said. "I don't want to be the cause of a tragedy."

"The big one will be on the sandbar tomorrow and we can get him."

"What will happen to this croc?" I asked.

"He will be eaten by his friends tonight," Adrian said. "We have plenty of crocodiles."

We headed for camp with the intention of returning early the next morning to see if we could kill the big crocodile. But when we left camp at dawn one of the boys saw a bush pig run off into the forest. After about two hours of hunting we came upon the pig. He was a fine specimen for my collection. We returned to camp to have him skinned out and salted down.

It was late in the afternoon when we finally approached the point where we had seen the big croc. We approached at a little different angle this time, moving directly in front of the sandbar. Adrian took a quick look with his binoculars while I kept my head down. "He's there," he said. "This one is very large in body size."

We crawled on our bellies for about 50 yards to the last line of grass. Then I lifted my rifle clear of the ground, centered the cross hairs on the monstrous head on a line between the two knots and pulled the trigger. "You got him," Adrian said. "He didn't even move."

We both raised up, got to our feet, and heard a chuckle behind us where the gun bearer had waited. At the same time we both realized that I had shot the same crocodile in the head I had killed the day before. "I can always take a joke, even when it is on me," I said to Adrian. "No wonder he had such a hell of a big head. He is really swollen."

"I could not see the length of him as we came upon him head-on," he said defensively.

"Don't worry about it," I said. "It's a good joke."

"I won't tell anyone if you won't," Adrian said. And until now I never have.

The nineteenth day of our hunt finally rolled around. All that day I was thinking about the big red puku on the long point, wondering if we should take him. We had not found another specimen as good. I mentioned my thoughts to Adrian on our way back to camp. "We will take him tomorrow morning," he promised.

We arrived at camp at sundown. Dante and Angelo were already there. Dante greeted me by saying, "We sure shot a big puku this evening."

I exchanged glances with Adrian and he asked, "Where did you shoot this puku?"

"At the long point of land," he answered. "You know the place."

"Dammit Dante, you shot my puku," I said.

"I didn't know it," Dante protested.

"I know you didn't," I said, "but we have been aware of that one since the second day here. We just wanted to be sure he was the best one around."

"I am sorry," Dante said. "I would not have killed it had I known."

"No problem," I said. "Did it make the book?"

"He went 18 and a quarter. Would that put him in the book?"

"It sure as hell would, with an inch and a quarter to spare," I said. "Let that be a lesson to both you and I, Adrian. Don't wait if you find a good

Two young women of Zambia keep a watchful eye on their children.

head."

So I came away from Zambia with only two trophies that made the record book, a wildebeest and a bush pig. This is the smallest number of record book trophies I have ever taken on a safari.

In my opinion, the reason that I only took two record book heads is because the Laungwa Valley is too well hunted to allow game to grow to record book size. In 16 years it has been cropped constantly. There is a lot of game to be had there and a beautiful country to hunt, but if you are looking for record book heads, you won't find them here.

14

Air safari in Ethiopia

Three years after my first hunt in Ethiopia, I again visited this fascinating country. This time I was accompanied by my wife Alvie.

Karl Luthy had visited us in California and stayed at our home while he was in the Los Angeles area. While there he talked of a beautiful area along the Omo River in the south of Ethiopia that was virtually untouched by civilization. This area is so remote that one must either fly from Addis Ababa over a high range of mountains that cross Ethiopia, or come up from Kenya through the Turkana Desert country. The Kenya route also presents a problem because the border between the two countries has always been a touchy location.

Karl told us that he had purchased a small airplane and would fly us in from Addis Ababa to a place called Murle where he had built a short landing strip. He even promised Alvie that he would build her a rondaavel on the bank of the Omo River because she did not care for a tent. Karl and I also discussed the hard to get trophies, such as Swaynes hartebeest, Tora hartebeest, Soemmerring gazelle, taing and other species that could only be taken in Ethiopia.

Alvie agreed to go, stay ten days and then return home. Karl and I were to

Opening pages: A low flying plane scatters a group of Thompson gazelle. Opposite page: A big waterbuck breaks away from the herd and stands alone.

My wife Alvie looks prepared for the safari.

hunt another fifteen days using the small airplane to move about the country. Air transportation is a necessity in order to collect some rare species that have scattered throughout the large territory.

The trip to Ethiopia was uneventful. Alvie and I spent two days in Addis Ababa, then flew out across the mountain range the next morning to Murle on a bank of the Omo River.

The air above the mountains is constantly filled with sand and small particles of dust rising up from the continuous burning of the thick brush that covers the mountains below. The local natives are always burning this bush off so they can cultivate the hills. This is done by using a terrace or contour type of field, plowing the furrows in a circular fashion around the hills so they catch and hold most of the sparse rainfall.

We saw many small patches of bananas shining like green jewels in the brown brush that surrounded them. The round thatched roofs of several small houses or rondaavels were always near these tiny cultivated plots of ground.

Murle contained a short landing strip near the bank of the Omo River. There were no buildings visible except Karl's camp, set on a high bank overlooking the muddy Omo. I understood that this strip serviced another such camp run by Ted Shatto and a small missionary settlement further down the river.

It was a beautiful area that resembled the region around Isiola Kenya. When the plane landed, a small herd of gazelle spooked and ran from the shade of one tree to another. Then they stood looking at us with large, limpid brown eyes, their ears cocked forward.

Overhead the ever present vultures circled high in the air. Two Land Rovers appeared from the clump of trees along the river. Young Peter Luthy and another young man named Eric got out of the vehicles and began loading our luggage and provisions into the two vehicles. We departed for the camp that was less than a mile away.

The camp was very comfortable and consisted of a large dining room with adjoining kitchen, several tents and a rondaavel that was not quite completed. It did not have a door and the plaster was still wet.

Karl had partially kept his promise to Alvie — the top and sides were up, but it had no door. We moved our gear into a tent while Karl apologized profusely for the uncompleted structure, blaming it on the incompetence of his staff.

Alvie and I went out to a small arbor covered by a roof of palm fronds. We sat down at a table overlooking the river below.

Our personal boy, Abdou, rushed to bring us cold beer and Tang from the oil-burning refrigerator. He also served cookies that he swore he had made himself.

We looked down on the slow-moving Omo and saw the head of hippo protruding from the water. Three crocodile lay on a sandbar further up the river. They had their mouths open and were getting their jaws cleaned of parasites by small white birds that jumped in and out among the jagged teeth. It was a peaceful scene and one that we were to enjoy for the next ten days. The location was especially enjoyable early in the morning and late in the afternoon when other animals came down to the river to drink.

We had an early dinner and turned in to the lonely wail of a foraging hyena. Late that night I was awakened by the roar of a distant lion.

We were again back in the land I had come to love.

Next morning we left the camp early and drove along the river. I have never seen so many herds of animal, except on the Sergangetti plains, as we saw that morning coming from the river where they had been watering.

Herds of Northern Grants gazelle came in a stream. The taing, with beautiful, dark reddish brown skin looking like rich velvet, numbered in the hundreds. As far as you could see, the land was dotted by these animals. Karl said the females were starting to drop their calves. Sure enough, a short time later we came upon several cows that had just given birth to wobbly calves.

"Thousands of taing come here to birth their calves," Karl said.

"Does it happen at the same time each year?" Alvie asked.

"You could almost mark your calendar on the day it will start," Karl answered. "In a week it is all over and they will start to migrate from here."

We saw thousands of small calves the next few days. The vultures, jackals and even the natives from nearby villages had a field day.

The vultures would sometimes attack the newborn calf. Even though the cow tried to protect it, there were a lot of vultures. Many times she lost the battle. The jackals simply ran in, snatched the newborn calf and ran off into the bush with it.

The blacks used clubs to kill the young calves. One man would carry several back to his village. It was a sad sight but one that took place only once each year.

On the first day out, an unusual event happened that almost sent Alvie back to Addis Ababa. We were traveling across the plains looking for animals with outstanding horns when we saw the figure of a man in the distance. Karl turned the car and headed in his direction. Quite often when on safari the professional hunter will stop a native and inquire about lion, leopard, elephant or other animals being hunted.

When we came to the man I was astonished to see that he was stark naked and carried only a spear in his hand. When Karl saw this he immediately veered the car away from the man and we continued on our way.

"What the hell is wrong with that man that he goes around naked?" I asked.

"You will see plenty like him before you leave," Karl answered. "These are the hammer people and one of the most primitive in Africa. They say it is too hot to wear clothes."

At about one P.M. in the heat of the day we returned to the camp. Again Alvie and I got a shock as most of the men in camp were walking around nude.

"Tell those men to get some clothes on," I ordered Karl. "And tell them that they damn well better be covered while the Memsabib is in camp."

Karl complied with the order. Several times when we came into camp in the heat of the day, many men would bolt for the single cloth that they wore draped over one shoulder. It covered the front of their crotch although sometimes their buttocks were still bare.

In four days of hunting I took some very fine animals. There were two Northern Grants gazelle that went in the record book plus two taing that were very high in the book. A Beisa oryx was also near the top in Rowland Wards.

Karl was right about the taing. In five days they were through calving as if someone had given an order. The huge herd suddenly vanished overnight, leaving only a few stragglers behind. It is still an age-old mystery why animals gather in one spot, then suddenly disappear.

We drove down toward Lake Rudoff to visit the village of the hammer people. Alvie and I found the tribe most interesting.

Like most natives in Africa, the hammer people use cattle as money and must, out of necessity, provide them with water.

It was the dry time of the year. When we arrived they were watering their cattle. There was no running water or even any pools of water where we found them.

I had seen the method used years before in old Tanganyika. Here the procedure was the same. A hole approximately 10 x 15 feet wide had been dug in the riverbed to a depth of 14 to 20 feet deep. Shelves were cut into the

Alvie poses with a good Ethiopian waterbuck.

sides at about five-foot intervals for the men to stand on. Near one end of this hole, a large trough made from the trunk of a tree lay with one end almost touching the hole in the ground. A narrow corral of poles had been fashioned so that not more than three or four cows could get water at a time. It took three men to make this system work and all were naked. The first stood in the water at the bottom of the pit. The next stood on a shelf five feet above him and the third five feet below the surface of the streambed.

The cows stood in a herd, held in check by men and boys about a hundred yards from the watering location. At intervals of a few minutes, three or four cows were allowed to go forward and enter the narrow corral where the trough lay. The water was lifted up in a chain reaction, first by the man at the bottom to the second and finally to the third man who emptied the bucket's contents into the trough. The cattle drank greedily, each pushing his nose as far as possible trying to get all the water up his throat in the short time allowed. After a few moments they were driven away by a brawny man with a club as another three or four animals advanced to drink.

The sweat poured from the lean bodies of the men working in the well and dripped into the water below. This, of course, was the same water the people had to drink. Occasionally a woman would come down the river bank with a pot on her head, dip it into the trough and depart up the bank again.

The country in this area was more arid than the land along the Omo River. I asked Karl why the hammer people didn't move and use the water from the Omo for their cows.

He replied that they had tried to do this several times, but it always resulted in a battle because another tribe claimed the land along the Omo. The primitive man is no different than the civilized man in this respect.

I took two fine Northern gerenuk and two Cordeaux dik-dik in this area, and they all made the record book. It seemed that everything I shot made the book because the area had rarely been hunted. We returned to our camp on the Omo which pleased Alvie very much.

I was very surprised that I saw no evidence of leopard along the Omo. There was also very little sign of lion although I heard the beast roar two or three times. We did not bait for either animal.

At the end of ten days, my wife departed for home. Karl and I were then met by another professional hunter, Roger McKay. He had joined us to fly

Karl's small plane on our air safari.

Ethiopia is a large country and traveling by road from one point to another would take too much time. In some cases, it would be nearly impossible. We planned to cover all these points by air, knowing that each town of any size had an Army base and a landing strip to service the installation.

The game department was our first stop. After some discussion, I was given a letter to the effect that I could take any species of game that was not on the endangered list. This gave me permission to hunt any location in Ethiopia.

Next we went to the Army commanding general of all Ethiopia. We requested a letter to any Army post commander to cooperate with us by providing an Army vehicle and driver if we paid for the petrol and the man's time.

Armed with these two important documents, we loaded our small airplane and headed for Dire Dawa to try to take an animal called the Sudan Soemmerring's gazelle.

In due time we arrived in Dire Dawa and found the commanding officer very cooperative. We had our American jeep and driver within an hour and were on our way to hunt.

Another hour and some thirty miles later, we located a herd of Soemmerring's gazelle. It was a quick stalk over the rolling terrain dotted with small bushes that resulted in a fine buck.

After putting him in the jeep, we followed the herd once again and shot another good buck. One measured 20-5/8 inches and the other 18¼ inches. These animals were quite tame and showed little evidence of hunting pressure.

We returned the jeep and driver at the end of the day, paid the officer in charge, added a nice tip and checked into the local rest house. The start of our air safari had been very successful.

We flew around Ethiopia for six days, stopping at Neghalli and Moyale where I collected good specimens of Borani Soemmerring's gazelle.

It would have taken us sixty days to cover this distance by jeep or Land Rover. The red tape with the local chieftans in each village would have been very difficult and extremely costly.

We returned to Addis Ababa to spend the day while Karl took care of business. We also needed a generator and other small ignition parts for an automobile. I will say one thing for Karl Luthy. He is a genius with motors and can repair almost any engine and get it running in a short time.

Our next destination was Gambella, a town that I had visited two years ago on my first safari to Ethiopia. However, this time we planned to fly the small plane down instead of taking the commercial airplane which flew there once a week.

We planned to leave early in the morning while the air was cool. In the middle of the day it would get hot because the airport at Addis Ababa is only 7,000 feet above sea level. We were heavily loaded with three big men, our gear, plus the added weight of a generator and other automobile parts. However, Karl continued to procrastinate, and it was noon before we arrived at the airport.

We loaded the small plane, got in and taxied down to the end of the runway. In the distance, several men were working behind a wooden barricade at the end of the runway. Roger gunned the little engine as the plane moved down the runway, its throttle completely open.

After going about 100 yards, Roger pulled back on the stick. The tail slowly came off the ground but the plane couldn't lift off the concrete. He pushed the stick forward for a moment, then brought it back sharply. Again the tail barely lifted. The end of the runway was approaching rapidly and I could see the men watching us bear down on them.

Once again Roger tried to lift the small plane off in the thin air. When it did not lift, he cut the throttle and applied the brakes. It was too late. The men scrambled for safety as we hit the barricade with our left wing. Roger hit the right rudder, placing equal pressure on that side. His alertness kept us out of the hole in the concrete. The left wing crashed through the light wood barricade as the plane continued to roll until it finally stopped on the grass at the end of the runway.

"Yegus Christ, that was close," Karl said. His English would get a bit mixed up with his Swiss under strain or excitement.

"I told you we must get off before it got hot," Roger replied.

"I don't know who in the hell is at fault," I said, "but that's a damn good way to get us killed."

We got out and inspected the plane but found little damage. The left landing light had been knocked off and a big dent was in the wing.

Roger shook the wing, thumped it a few times and announced, "She's OK, nothing damaged."

We again got into the plane while the Ethiopian workmen jabbered among themselves. They remained a good distance from both the airplane and the pit in the ground until we were well away, taxiing back to the airport.

It was decided we should wait until the next morning to try it again. Roger was arguing that we were overloaded, and Karl was adamant that he needed everything that was in the airplane.

I declined to leave one of my rifles behind. I had a .300 Weatherby and a .458 Browning that I felt I would need as I would be hunting buffalo and elephant. Both of the large animals can get a bit nasty in Ethiopia. Karl had a 9 MM which is considered very light for big game; Roger didn't have any rifle at all.

The next morning we were at the airport at daybreak. When it was light enough to see, we again taxied down to the end of the runway. I crossed my fingers as we roared down the strip. We lifted into the air before covering half its full distance.

It was a beautiful morning. The little plane hummed along leaving the big sprawling city of Addis behind. It floated over the cultivated land that surrounded the city and over the rolling hills of the bush country.

I watched the altimeter as the hand crept up to 8,000, then 9,000 feet. Finally when we reached 10,500 feet, we leveled off and everyone relaxed. However, something was nagging at my mind but I didn't know why I felt uneasy. The motor sounded good, the gas tanks showed full and all looked well.

"How are things going, Roger?" I asked.

"Everything's fine," he grinned, showing his crooked teeth. "Be in Gambella in about three and a half hours."

"That's about all the gas this will carry, isn't it?"

"We have enough for four hours."

"That doesn't give us much room for mistakes, does it?"

"Oh, we will follow the road," he said. "Look over the right side. Can't get lost, old boy."

Sure enough, down below was a thin ribbon of dirt that twisted and turned like a snake in torment. I remembered that it had taken Karl's young son, Peter, five days to drive from Addis to Gambella, and he had turned the jeep and iron trailer over twice on the way. I half dozed in the warm sunlight.

I must have slept for two hours before I was awakened by the feeling that the aircraft was turning. I opened my eyes and the first thing I saw was the peaks of a mountain range towering several hundred feet above us on the right side.

"What's wrong, Roger?" I asked.

"Got to get a bit more altitude to get over that range so I am spiraling."

So that's what was bothering me. I knew there was a high mountain range between Addis and Gambella and we should have been climbing to nearly 15,000 feet in order to clear them.

It was approaching noon and the air had heated up. I watched the altimeter as we spiraled. It moved very little and finally became still at 12,000 feet. "We are not climbing, Roger," I said.

"I know it," he answered. "She won't lift in this hot air."

I had a sinking feeling in the pit of my stomach.

"One tank is on empty and the other is at half full," I announced. "You better think of something."

"Mein Gott!" Karl said from the rear. He, too, had awakened.

"We will fly down this range until we come to a pass, then fly through it," Roger decided.

He turned the small airplane parallel with the mountain range and started flying alongside it. I don't know what the others were doing but I was alternately looking at the black rocks of the mountain peaks and the rough ground below. Unless we had some luck pretty soon, it would probably be our last resting place for a long time to come. There are no people in this desolate stretch of country, just rocks and scrub brush.

"There is a pass ahead," Roger announced suddenly.

Sure enough, a slot appeared between two tall peaks just below the altitude at which we were flying.

"What happens if we go in and it doesn't go through?" I asked.

He shrugged his shoulders, his voice was tense as he said, "We have no other choice."

The Good Lord must have had his hand on us that day as the opening wound through the mountains. The passage was wide enough for the small plane. We came out on the other side, turning back in the direction we had been flying on the other side of the range. This time we angled away from the mountain.

It was another 30 minutes before I spotted our salvation.

"Roger, look! A landing strip below!"

"Must be a mission," he replied. "Ten minutes more and we will be at the river."

"But the gas gauge shows empty. Let's set it down."

We hit the ground with a bounce; the engine coughed and quit. The plane rolled to a stop. We all just sat there without moving for a few minutes.

"Well, we made it," Roger cracked the silence.

"You dumb bastard, there's no way I will ever fly with you again."

"Better than walking, old chap," he grinned.

He was not offended. He knew he had made a serious error and only by sheer luck had we survived.

The father of the mission walked down the field, followed by his parishioners and stood waiting for us to climb down from the plane.

I climbed out followed by Roger and Karl. We introduced ourselves to the priest. After explaining our predicament we managed to wrangle five gallons of gas from him. That is all he could give. It would be plenty to make the 40 miles into Gambella.

We stayed the night in order to take off while it was cool. Without the weight of two full tanks of gas, we would be much lighter.

The next morning we pulled the plane to the farthest end of the strip, even putting the tail into the bushes just to be safe. We climbed in and Roger revved the motor up full blast while stepping on the brake. Then he let go the brakes and we went bouncing down the strip.

We arrived in Gambella a few minutes later and landed at the public airport. I have never been so glad to see one.

We were fortunate in getting a ride into town with all our gear. We checked into one of the bug-ridden guest houses near the river. I stayed with the guns while Karl and Roger crossed the river to work on the car that Karl had left some three years before.

Karl and Roger returned that evening. Roger took me aside while Karl went to the room.

"Mac, you'd better look at that car before we go into the bush with it."

"What's wrong with it?"

"Don't say I said so, but go with Karl tomorrow morning and I will stay with the guns."

He wouldn't say any more, but I feared the worst.

In the morning I told Karl I wanted to go across the river with him. After arguing about it, he agreed.

The log dugout quickly took us across the river and we landed at the same place that we had unloaded the jeep over three years before.

I followed Karl up to a native hut where some scrawny chickens were scratching in the earth and a flea-bitten dog started yapping at us. The door was made of split bamboo and hung on leather hinges. It swung open and a handsome Ethiopian with classical features came out.

Karl introduced the young man as "Peter."

Both Peter and I followed Karl out to the large spreading tree. Karl stopped beside the most beat-up pile of tin and iron in the form of an automobile that I have ever seen.

It was once a touring car with a cloth roof. That had been destroyed many years ago. Both headlights had been knocked out. The cotton padding and springs were showing through the upholstered backs and seats. There was not a fender that was not bent; the whole body was encrusted with rust.

"Karl, would you actually go into the bush in this thing?"

"Why not? I can get it running. It ran good three years ago."

Karl knocked off at noon. We crossed over the river and walked up to a small store where one could buy almost anything. I was hoping the man would have some tires that would fit Karl's wonderful machine. They didn't, so we bought two bottles of Coke while Karl was figuring what supplies we would need for a nine-day safari.

I was sitting, thinking how I managed to get into my present position when a voice spoke that I recognized.

"Hello Mac, what are you doing back in Ethiopia?"

I turned around and shook hands with Tom Mattanovich, another professional hunter from Addis Ababa.

"I am back to pick up some animals I didn't take on the first trip," I told him.

"Tom, do you have a vehicle across the river?" I asked.

"A brand new Toyota," he answered. The Good Lord was smiling again.

"Would you consider renting your Toyota for nine days?"

"Not unless I drove it."

"You are on," I agreed, and we shook hands on the deal just as Karl came out of the store. Tom walked into the store to get his supplies while Karl and I started down to the rest house where Roger was waiting.

Waterbuck was one of the top game in Ethiopia. This one measured a fine 32 inches of horn.

"I just rented Tom's new Toyota," I said as we walked along.

Karl stopped and said, "We have a car."

"I know, but this is a good car and we need one back in that rough country."

"I am the professional hunter and I will make the decisions," he said stubbornly.

"You will, like hell, on this matter. You know that car of yours is in no shape to go back in the bush."

"Who will pay Mattanovich?"

"I will pay him, you and Roger on the same basis that we agreed. There is no difference. You are still the professional hunter and Tom will be the driver." We reached the hotel and I told Roger about the Toyota. I could tell that Roger was very pleased with the new setup, but Karl turned sullen, determined not to cooperate at all.

The next nine days were, without a doubt, the most miserable I have spent on safari. Every day was boiling hot without a cloud in the sky. At night we slept where we could which was usually on the ground. We were bitten all night by mosquitos, in spite of the Off mosquito repellent I used. The friction between the two professionals hung like a cloud over us all.

I shot roan, hartebeest, and wart hog while searching for the elusive northeastern buffalo that I wanted most of all. The hunting was bad, and we saw very few animals in the huge area we covered. Then on the seventh day of the hunt we got the break we needed.

We were riding along in a thickly wooded area when Roger touched me on the shoulder and whispered, "Buffalo."

Tom stopped the Toyota, and Roger pointed in the direction of a large

Despite our difficulties in the air over Ethiopia, we managed to do alright on the ground as shown by this trophy.

patch of tall grass. Standing under a bush was a lone bull about 100 yards from the seven-foot-high grass.

Tom and I took one look through our binoculars and piled out of the vehicle. We went creeping forward, Tom with his .375 and I with my .458.

The bull was standing with his rear to us and appeared to be dozing in the heat of the day. I knew that we would be extremely lucky if we could get in a position for a good shot without him hearing or seeing us. There was very little cover.

I angled toward his right side, aware that I must get in a location where I could at least see his shoulder. I was hoping for an angled shot into his rib section and into the chest cavity. Tom and I moved as softly as we could over the dry ground. I was almost where I had hoped to be when the bull suddenly turned his head and looked at us. I threw up my rifle and snapped off a shot toward his rib section.

I heard the solid contact with the bull. He lunged forward into the tall grass in front of him.

"You hit him a little far back," Tom said.

"I think you are right, but I believe it was a killing shot," I answered.

Tom shook his head, "I don't believe so."

Karl had left the car carrying his 9 MM gun. Roger had my 16 mm K100 camera in his hand. "I came up to take the action," he said grinning.

"Damn little action you are going to see in that tall grass," I replied.

"I'm going to climb a tree," he answered. All four of us cautiously approached the tall grass as Tom moved to my left about 20 feet. Karl followed while Tom and I walked quietly into the grass. It was plain to see that Karl was not too happy to go into the grass with us.

I don't suppose one could blame him. A 9 MM is a light gun for a wounded buffalo. However, I had warned him about taking this light gun, but he wouldn't listen.

So Tom and I walked into the grass, Karl stopped at the edge. I held my rifle waist high to keep the grass out of my face and, at the same time, be ready for action. We moved a step at a time and had penetrated about 30 feet into the grass when Roger's voice rang out from above.

"To your right, Mac," he shouted, "To your right."

I swung to my right and I could only see a dark bulk in the yellow grass. I put a .458 solid into the middle of the dark spot as Tom's .375 roared on my left. I threw out the empty and shot again into the now churning figure in front of me. Tom also took a second shot.

When I shot a third time, the bull bawled and hit the ground. He was through. Both Tom and I approached carefully; the bull jerked feebly so Tom put a bullet in his neck, just to make sure.

We shook hands over the dead buffalo with a feeling of mutual respect. Karl came forward, followed by Roger. I am sure Roger saved me from a battering from the buffalo. Had Tom and I walked farther, I would have been in his line of fire, or perhaps I would not have been able to stop his charge when the animal came. Tom and I worked late that night caping out the huge head of the bull. The next day we returned to the river and Gambella with the trophies that I wanted from this area.

I paid Tom before the three of us flew back to Gambella on the commercial flight. There was no aviation gasoline in Gambella for the small plane. In a way I was glad because I did not want to fly in the small plane again. There is such a thing as stretching your luck.

I left Ethiopia feeling that I had hunted the country as thoroughly as anyone could on an air safari.